高职高专"十一五"规划教材

电子商务专业英语

徐晓冬　主　编

曾祥娟　金　郁　副主编

化学工业出版社

·北京·

本书的编写始终贯穿着一切从实用出发的理念,在文章内容、教学要求和信函的写作技巧等方面皆有所创新,并列举了大量来自实际电子商务活动中的原生态选材,包括电子商务的历史、商业模式、成功案例故事、运营机制、发展展望以及网上开店与购物等多方面内容,新颖独特,实践性强,简捷易学。有助于提高学生阅读英文网站的水平和理解英文网站的组织结构,以及如何地道的使用英语处理电子商务活动中的 E-mail、Complain 等相关业务。

　　主要适合于高职高专电子商务、国际贸易等专业师生使用,也可以供电子商务及相关专业从业人员的在职培训和自修提高之用。

图书在版编目(CIP)数据

电子商务专业英语/徐晓冬主编 . —北京:化学工业
出版社,2008.5
高职高专"十一五"规划教材
ISBN 978-7-122-02517-3

Ⅰ. 电… Ⅱ. 徐… Ⅲ. 电子商务-英语-高等学校:
技术学院-教材 Ⅳ. H31

中国版本图书馆 CIP 数据核字(2008)第 053820 号

责任编辑:李彦玲　于　卉　　　　　　　　装帧设计:于　兵
责任校对:蒋　宇

出版发行:化学工业出版社(北京市东城区青年湖南街 13 号　邮政编码 100011)
印　　装:北京云浩印刷有限责任公司
787mm×1092mm　1/16　印张 6½　字数 131 千字　2008 年 7 月北京第 1 版第 1 次印刷

购书咨询:010-64518888(传真:010-64519686)　售后服务:010-64518899
网　　址:http://www.cip.com.cn
凡购买本书,如有缺损质量问题,本社销售中心负责调换。

定　价:14.00 元

前　言

E-commerce 这个十年前我们对它还一无所知或者说知之甚少的名词，今天不但家喻户晓，而且还渗透在我们生活的各个方面，完全彻底地改变了我们长期以来一直认为是天经地义的这个世界的经济运行模式，带给我们全球化经济的新视点（The world is flat）。我们所有的人都无一例外的置身其中目睹着这场变革，并在变革中重新寻找和认识我们自己的价值。

经济全球化最值得关注的特点之一，就是全世界素不相识的企业和个人，哪怕你是在最偏远的角落，都愉快地聚集在一个世界级的 "Shopping Mall" 里自由地选择他们所需要的交易。尽管他们来自不同的国度，操不同的语言，但至少有一种语言可以使他们彼此相通，那就是 E-commerce English。

E-commerce English 是 Internet 商务活动中获取更多商业机会和信息的工具，只要你期望成为 E-commerce 的成功者，就没有理由拒绝学习和掌握它。本书主要为高等学校电子商务专业的学生以及目前社会所亟需的电子商务人才学习使用，帮助他们提高阅读英文网页的水平和理解英文网站的组织结构，以及如何地道地使用英语处理电子商务活动中的相关业务。

参加本教材编写的人员大都从事过电子商务英语的教学活动，并且在国际化的电子商务实践中积累了丰富的实战经验，并取得了一定的研究成果。他们分别来自国防科技大学、河南工程学院、内蒙古化工学院、山东第二技术学院、辽宁信息职业技术学院和科晶集团公司。其中第 1，2，4，12 章及本书的电子邮件部分由徐晓冬、曾祥娟编写，第 3，11 章由屈婷婷编写，第 5 章由刘伟编写，第 6，8 章由宓淑环编写，第 7，9，10 章由金郁编写。此外我们还要特别感谢科晶集团公司和美国 MTI 公司提供的 E-mail 信函资料，这些资料都是在实际应用当中节选出来的。

由于编者的知识及时间有限，书中难免存在不足之处，敬请专家与读者批评指正。

编者
2008 年 4 月

Table of Contents

Unit 1   Going Close to E-commerce

Warming-up Questions:
1. How much do you know about e-commerce?
2. Can you name some words which are Internet-related?
3. Do you think e-commerce is far away from us?

Related links:
1. http://www. managementhelp. org/infomgnt/e _cmmrce/e _cmmrce. htm
#anchor1167431
2. http://www. ecommercetimes. com/perl/section/ebiz/

When talking about e-commerce, people always try to define it in a definite way. In fact, unlike some definitions in natural science, we can hardly find an exact and accurate definition to explain e-commerce because of its spectacular impacts on human beings' activities and of its fast growing. Actually in today's Internet-based society, e-commerce is an indispensable part of our life, and we are experiencing the great changes it has brought about to our daily lives. The management guru, Peter Drucker, once describes e-commerce in such words: *The truly revolutionary impact of the Internet Revolution is just beginning to be felt. But it is not "information" that fuels this impact. It is not "artificial intelligence", It is not the effect of computers and data processing on decision making, policymaking, or strategy. It is something that practically no one foresaw or, indeed even talked about 10 or 15 years ago; e-commerce—that is, the explosive emergence of the Internet as a major, perhaps eventually the major, worldwide distribution channel for goods, for services, and, surprisingly, for managerial and professional jobs. This is profoundly changing economics, markets and industry structure, products and services and their flow; consumer segmentation, consumer values and consumer behavior; jobs and labor markets. But the impact may be even greater on societies and politics, and above all, on the way we see the world and ourselves in it.* It, therefore, is less meaningful for us to define e-commerce. Probably the definition we give today will become obsolete tomorrow or even at next minute.

E-commerce—It's More Than Buying and Selling

E-commerce, also known as e-business, describes the manner in which trans-

Remark

actions take place over networks, mostly the Internet. It is the process of electronically buying and selling goods, services, and information. Certain e-commerce applications, such as buying and selling stocks on the Internet, are growing very rapidly. But e-commerce is not just about buying and selling; it is also about electronically communicating, collaborating, and discovering information. It is about e-learning, e-government, and much more. E-commerce will impact a significant portion of the world, affecting business, professions, and of course, people.

Although the features of e-commerce include all types of activities, they can be put into two categories: (1) the online sale of goods or services and (2) the online distribution of information. Some authorities use the term electronic commerce or e-commerce to mean buying and selling goods and services over the Internet. But we prefer to use a broader explanation: e-commerce is any electronic exchange of information to conduct business.

The Interdisciplinary Nature of E-commerce

As a new disciplinary field, e-commerce is just now developing its theoretical and scientific foundations. But today, in the academic field, it is widely accepted that e-commerce is only a means by which people can get related information rather than a discipline worthy of studying and researching. Actually in modern society, we are so dependable on e-commerce You can probably see that EC is related to many different disciplines, including Computer Science, Marketing , Consumer Behavior, Finance, Economics, Management Information Systems, Business Law, and Engineering.

The Partnership Between the Internet and Business

It, to entrepreneurs, is an everlasting topic to gain the maximum profit at the cost as low as possible. A business can open a Web storefront in the local area and find the world at its doorstep. The easiest way to understand the close alliance between the internet and business is to search the Internet itself. Popular search engines, such as Yahoo, Google and Baidu, show categories for business and related subjects. Some provide immediate links to business topics, where customers can easily find the products quotation or company names on their flashing screens. As you have seen, companies use the Web to sell products and services and to make information available. E-commerce can help them control costs by not having to print and mail catalogs and brochures. They can advertise and communicate on the Web, reaching a worldwide audience that they might never be able to reach otherwise.

Remark

They can make themselves available to customers 24 hours a day，7 days a week.

Words and Expressions

spectacular *adj.*	unusually great	巨大的
impact *n.*	影响	
indispensable *adj.*	essential，important	关键的，不可缺少的
guru *n.*	专家，权威	
artificial intelligence	人工智能	
practically *adv.*	almost or very nearly	几乎
managerial *adj.*	管理的	
segmentation *n.*	分割，分离	
transaction *n.*	doing and completing a business activity	交易
collaborate *v.*	合作	
entrepreneur *n.*	企业家	
quotation *n.*	报价	
brochure *n.*	小册子	

Notes

1. **Peter Ferdinand Drucker** （November 19，1909～November 11，2005） was a voice for change and new ways of thinking about social and business relations . Drucker was born in a suburb of Vienna in a small village named Kaasgraben （nowadays part of the 19th district，Döbling）. He earned a doctorate in International Law. In 1943，he became a naturalized citizen of the United States. He taught at New York University as Professor of Management from 1950 to 1971. From 1971 to his death he was the Clarke Professor of Social Science and Management at Claremont Graduate University.

2. **Yahoo，Google and Baidu：** widely used search engines for the web that finds information，news，images，products，finance. Nowadays these words are frequently used in our daily lives and some words have been given new meanings. For example，my children are googling all the day.

Exercises

Reading Comprehension

According to the text，answer the following questions.

1. According to the text，what does e-commerce mean?

2. How do you understand the quotation cited from Peter Drucker?

3. How do you understand the relationship between business and the Internet?

Remark

4. Do you agree with the author's statement that e-commerce has brought about great changes to our lives? If yes, can you give some examples?

5. What does the sentence "e-commerce is any electronic exchange of information to conduct business" mean?

Translation

A. Translate the following sentences into Chinese.

1. It is something that practically no one foresaw or, indeed even talked about 10 or 15 years ago: e-commerce—that is, the explosive emergence of the Internet as a major, perhaps eventually the major, worldwide distribution channel for goods, for services, and, surprisingly, for managerial and professional jobs.

2. But today, in the academic field, it is widely accepted that e-commerce is only a means by which people can get related information rather than a discipline worthy of studying and researching.

3. They can advertise and communicate on the Web, reaching a worldwide audience that they might never be able to reach otherwise.

4. The easiest way to understand the close alliance between the internet and business is to search the Internet itself.

5. Some provide immediate links to business topics, where customers can easily find the products quotation or company names on their flashing screens.

B. Translate the following sentences into English with the given words or expressions.

1. 关于电子商务的定义，我们更倾向于使用更为宽泛的一种解释方法，那就是，在进行贸易时任何信息的交换。(prefer to)

2. 在网络快速普及的今天，我们可以说电子商务是人们生活中不可或缺的。(indispensable)

3. 如果有现货的话，可以立即发货。(available)

4. 所有的贸易往来都是通过网络实现的。(take place)

5. 电子商务给个人、机构带来的影响是无法估量的。(impact)

Supplementary Reading

E-commerce —Advantages

The advantages of E-commerce are basically increased sales and decreased costs through the use of electronical media, especially the Web. The advantages of E-commerce will be divided into the benefits it provides to organizations, consumers, and society.

Advantages to Organizations

Due to the global reach of the Internet, businesses organizations are able to send messages worldwide, exploring new markets and opportunities. This breaks down geographic limitations, and reaches narrow markets that traditional businesses have difficulties accessing. Through the Internet, business now offer a wide range of choices and higher levels of customer information and details for individuals to search and compare. Some build-to-order companies such as Dell Computer Corp can even provide a competitive advantage by inexpensive customization of products and services.

In terms of cost reduction, E-commerce helps organizations decrease costs in creating, processing, distributing, storing and retrieving information. For example the communication and advertising costs could be lowered by sending e-mails and using online advertising channels, than by using television commercials or the print media. In terms of online ordering and online auction organizations, the costs could be lower than running an actual shop with the associated manpower.

Extended trading hours is another benefit, the 24 hours a day. 7 days a week in 365 days allows business always free to open on the Internet without overtime and extra cost. Other advantages includes the up-to-date company material, current inventories, improved customers service, better customers communication, increased operating and trading flexibility

Advantages to Consumers

For customers, the advantages occur in the buying process, product research, evaluation and execution. E-commerce provides customers with a platform to search product information through global markets with a wider range of choices, which makes comparison and evaluation easier and more efficient. With the ubiquity in accessing the Internet, consumers are able to search for shops or perform other transactions anytime in almost any location. Cheaper goods and services is one of the benefits for consumers who purchase online. Furthermore, delivery time and costs can be saved by buyers when they purchase digital goods and services. Examples are e-books, music and audio clips, software, games, and distance education delivered via the Internet.

Advantages to Society

By telecommuting, individuals can nowadays work and do their purchasing at home rather than by traveling around. This will result in less traffic and air pollution. For people in developing countries, many services and products are now available which were unavailable in the past; opportunities and higher education services are more achievable for students. Non-profit organizations, including government services, also benefit from E-commerce by the online payment system which supports the payment of tax refunds and pensions quickly and securely. Public services such as health care, education, and public social service also benefit from E-commerce. For example, rural doctors and nurses can access professional information and the latest health care technologies. Overall, e-commerce makes products and services more easily available without geographic limitations.

Remark

Words and expressions

geographic limitation	地理局限性
access *v.*	接近、进入
manpower *n.*	人力
execution *n.*	实行、执行
platform *n.*	平台
ubiquity *n.*	独特性
transaction *n.*	交易
overall *adv.*	总体地

A Guide to E-mail Writting

实用电子商务信函

　　写作特点：E-mail 商业信函是简洁的，是不太讲究格式的，有时甚至是一两句话来完成的。但目的性很强。E-mail 信函的基本要素包括：①对象；②目的；③要求对方做什么或提供什么信息咨询；④发函人的联系方式，包括姓名、电话、Fax（方便传递合同）、地址，以便收信人掌握发函人的信息，进一步为发函人提供服务。

Specimen Letter

Hi　Moyi,

Please provide the quotation and delivery date：

1. Copper single crystal：

　　Dimension：25mm diameter by 1mm thick or thinner.

　　Available orientation，Quantity：6 pieces

2. Gold single crystal：

　　Orientation：111

　　Dimension：1 mm diameter by 5 mm long

　　Quantity：1 pieces

Thanks.

Byron

MTI Corporation

World leader for Advanced crystal and Lab equipment

Phone：510-525-3070

Fax：510-525-4705

E-mail：sales@mticrystal.com

Website：www.mtixtl.com

　　点评：从上面的信函可以看出，询价方与供货方是一种长期的合作关系，因为开始的称呼很随便没有太多的礼节性语言。目的性很强，要求对方提供报价和交货期。例如，available orientation 显然是在问供方能够提供的晶向。信的内容专业性很强，是询问铜单晶和金单晶材料以及相关的技术要求和数量。

Remark

<table>
<tr><td>Unit 2</td><td>A Brief History of E-Commerce and EDI Standard</td></tr>
</table>

Warming-up Questions:

1. How do we understand the saying that "The world is flat"?

2. Undoubtedly, with the popularity of the Internet, e-commerce has penetrated into every corner of our life. Would you like to give some examples to illustrate how e-commerce influences your life?

3. What does EDI stand for and what role does it play in the development of E-commerce?

Related Links:

1. http://www.mapsofworld.com/referrals/internet/internet-history/history-of-e-commerce.htm

2. http://www.flysyk02.netfirms.com/Ecommerce/History.htm

E-commerce the magic thing, that practically no one knew or even talked about 17 years ago, becomes so popular that it has affected almost every detail of our life and totally changed the economic running model of the world which we think should be God's truth. As a result E-commerce brings us the new idea of global economy— " The world is flat " . All of us, with no exception, witness the great changes and reappraise the values of ourselves in the innovation.

Brief History of E-commerce

E-commerce applications were first developed in the early 1970s with innovations such as Electronic Funds Transfer (EFT) in which funds could be routed electronically from one organization to another. However, the extent of the applications was limited to large corporations, financial institutions, and a few other daring businesses. Then came Electronic Data Interchange (EDI), a technology used to electronically transfer routine documents, which expanded electronic transfers from financial transactions to other types of transaction processing (such as ordering, invoice receipts, shipping documents etc.). This new application enlarged the pool of participating companies from financial institutions to manufacturers, retailers, services, and many other types of businesses. More new EC applications followed, ranging from travel reservation systems to stock trading systems. Such

Remark

systems were called interorganizational system (IOS) application, and their strategic value to businesses has been widely recognized.

As we know, the development of EC is based on the growth of the Internet. The Internet began life as an experiment by the U. S. government in 1969, and its initial users were a largely technical audience of government agencies and academic researchers and scientists. When the Internet commercialized and users began flocking to participate in the World Wide Web in the early 1990s, the term electronic commerce was coined. As the EC applications rapidly expanded, a large number of so-called dot-coms, or Internet start-ups, also appeared. One reason for this rapid expansion was the development of new networks, protocols, and software. The other reason was the increase in competition and other business pressures.

EDI Standard

EDI (Electronic Data Interchange) is a communication standard that enables the electronic transfer of routine documents such as purchasing order, invoices, receipts, shipping documents between business partners. EDI often serves as catalyst and stimulus to improve the business processes that flow between organizations. It reduces costs, delays, and errors inherent in a manual document-delivery system. Therefore, it is important for us to understand how the EDI works and improves the development of E-commerce.

Problems Among the Traditional Information Interchange

Traditional information interchange between business partners mainly focused on replacing pre-defined or pre-printed business forms with similar defined electronic forms on computers, such as purchase orders, invoices, or delivery information. However, the procedures of processing those documents remain the same as before. For example, a typical purchasing system, which allows clients to review their material requirements and create purchase orders automatically according to stock levels and Bill of Materials (BOM). The created purchase order will be printed out and mailed to the supplier. The supplier then manually enters item information to their customer shipping system upon receiving the order. Information to be input may include customer names, order dates, order items, quantities, lead time, agreed price; payment methods and so on. On the date of delivery, ordered items will be shipped. Invoice will then be printed by the shipping system and mailed back to the purchaser.

As we can see in the example, even if the purchased items were ordered and

Remark

shipped on the same day, the lead time could be as much as a week or more. So it is obvious that the traditional information interchange protocol could result in the following problems.

• Long Processing Time

In the traditional paper-based processing system, the physical transmission of documents between trading partners caused the increase of processing time to complete a single transaction. Another reason which caused the processing time last longer is the time it takes to re-enter data. Same information is entered twice in the example above. However, the number of re-entering data will be a lot more in the real practices, especially in the manufacturing industries.

• Low Accuracy

Due to the paper-based system that requires multiple instances of the same information, data have to be re-entered at various places within the processing life cycle. Clearly, repeat entering the same data greatly increases the possibilities of errors.

• High Labor Cost

Traditional flow of information requires data to be entered manually at each step in the processing cycle and all these operations are labor intensive.

• Increased Uncertainty

Because of the delays in mailing and processing stage, the time of receiving document will be unsure. It is not unusual that a merchant find out that the supplier never received the purchase order when the items are not delivered as expected. This kind of uncertainty often resulted in constant telephoning to confirm the receipt of document.

Can EDI Solve the Problems?

The use of Electronic Data Interchange can help to eliminate or significantly reduce the problems found in the traditional information interchange system. For instance, with the implementation of EDI in the previous example, the merchant can still review their material requirements and create purchase orders. However instead of printing a hardcopy of the order and mailing it, the purchase order will be transmitted directly to the supplier over an electronic network.

On the supplier's end, the transaction will be received and posted automatical-

Remark

ly. If there is an available stock, the supplier can even deliver the items on the same date they received the order. Furthermore, the supplier now can send its shipping document and notification electronically to the merchant, enabling the client to accurately receive documents prior to the actual arrival of the items. In addition, since the invoice can be sent directly to the merchant's accounts payable system through the EDI implementation, the supplier can receive its payment sooner than before.

Consequently, most of the problems and drawbacks, which are encountered in the traditional system can be solved. With the implementation of EDI, the productivity, efficiency and accuracy between business and trading partners can be greatly improved.

How does EDI Work?

Normally, a typical EDI transaction needs to go five steps. These steps together with the EDI standards make the exchange of data possible between two trading partners.

Step1: Preparation of electronic documents

The first step is the collection of information and data. The way to collect the required information should be the same as the way to do it in the traditional system. The difference is the system has to build an electronic file or database to store those data.

Step2: Outbound translation

This step is to translate the electronic file or database into a standard format according to the specification of the corresponding document. The resulting data file should contain a series of structured transactions related to the purchase order for example. If more than one company is involved in the particular transaction individual files should be produced for each of them.

Step3: Communication

Then the computer should connect and transmit those data file to the pre-arranged Value Added Network (VAN) automatically. The VAN then process each file and route to the appropriate electronic mailboxes according to the destination set in the file.

Step4: Inbound translation

The destination company should be able to retrieve the file from their electronic mailboxes in a constant period, and then reverse the process by translating the file from the standard format into the specific format required by the company's application software.

Step5: Processing the electronic documents

Remark

The internal application system of the destination company can process the received documents now. All the resulted documents corresponding to the received transaction should use the same processes or steps to transmit back to the transaction initiator. The whole cycle of the electronic data interchange can then be completed.

The Benefits of EDI

- EDI enables companies to send and receive large amounts of routine transaction information quickly around the globe.
- Computer-to-computer data transfer reduces the number of errors.
- Information can flow among several trading partners consistently and freely.
- Companies can access partners' databases to retrieve and store standard transactions.
- EDI fosters true (and strategic) partnership/relationship because it involves a commitment to a long-term investment and the refinement of the system over time.
- EDI creates a complete paperless TPS (transaction processing system) environment, saving money and increasing efficiency.
- Payment collection can be shortened by several weeks.
- Data may be entered off-line, in a batch mode, without tying up ports to the mainframe.
- When an EDI document is received, the data may be used immediately.
- Sales information is delivered to manufactures, shippers, and warehouses almost in real time .
- EDI can save companies a considerable amount of money.

As more and more companies get connected to the Internet, EDI is becoming increasingly important as an easy mechanism for companies to buy, sell, and trade information.

Words and Expressions

practically *adv.*	almost or very nearly	差不多
God's truth	天经地义的	
witness *vt.*	目睹，目击	
reappraise *v.*	评价，估价，鉴定	
innovation *n.*	(the use of) a new idea or method	变革
EFT	电子资金转账	
routine *adj.*	a habitual or fixed way of doing things	常规的

Remark

inherent *adj.*	内在的，固有的
stimulus *n.*	刺激，激励
catalyst *n.*	催化剂
Dot-coms *n.*	网络公司
client *n.*	客户
lead time *n.*	交货期
pre-defined	预先确定的
Bill of Materials	材料单
labor intensive	劳动密集
accounts payable *n.*	应付款
consequently *adv.*	从而，因此
drawback *n.*	缺点，障碍
encounter *v.*	遭遇

Notes

1. **The world is flat**：世界是平的，是美国《纽约时报》专栏作家是托马斯·弗里德曼用了 4 年时间写成的一本重点论述"全球化"的专著。

2. **Value Added Network**（VAN）增值网络（是将通信线路租给订户的一种网络服务，它增加了额外的服务或功能，例如：安全性、错误检测、有保障的消息传递和消息缓冲区）

Exercises

Reading Comprehension

According to the text，answer the following questions.

1. How many stages are there in the development of e-commerce?

2. There is no doubt that the rapid development of EC can be mainly accounted to the fast growth of the Internet. Can you give some other reasons which contribute to the development of e-commerce?

3. What are the problems in the traditional information interchange?

4. Compared with the other standards，what are the advantages of EDI standard?

Translation

A. Translate the following sentences into Chinese.

1. This new application enlarged the pool of participating companies from financial institutions to manufacturers，retailers，services，and many other types of businesses.

2. In the traditional paper-based processing system，the physical transmission

Remark

of documents between trading partners caused the increase of processing time to complete a single transaction.

3. The destination company should be able to retrieve the file from their electronic mailboxes in a constant period, and then reverse the process by translating the file from the standard format into the specific format required by the company's application software.

B. Translate the following sentences into English with the given words or expressions.

1. 当商品没有如期运到时，商人发现供货商没有收到订单，这是很常见的事。(find out)

2. 传统的生意伙伴间信息交换主要集中在用相似的电子表格代替已经制定好的商业表格。(focus on)

3. EDI 常常用作催化剂来推动各机构间贸易进程。(serve as)

4. 在 20 世纪 90 年代初，当人们开始蜂拥使用网络时，电子商务这个术语便产生了。(participate in)

Supplementary Reading

The Short History of E-commerce

It seems that e-commerce has always been a part of our lives. Most of us make business transactions online on such a regular basis that it is difficult to imagine a time when you were not able to do so. Despite this, the history of e-commerce is actually a relatively short history. It began less than fifty years ago and its humble beginnings look nothing like the kind of electronic business transactions that we see today. Even up until the 1990's, online business wasn't a reality for the average person. So how did we get to the point where e-commerce has become practically a way of life?

The development of e-commerce was one of those things that happened slowly and then suddenly. At its very basic level, the term refers simply to any commerce that takes place electronically. This includes ATM and credit card transactions as well as the ability to do billing and invoicing through electronic methods. The technology allowing this kind of commerce took place in the late 1970's and grew steadily throughout the 1980's. It was during this time that people started to use credit cards on a regular basis and that set the foundation for electronic commerce to get a toehold in society.

However, it wasn't until the development of the Internet that e-commerce started looking like the type of business that we know today. For most people talking about it now, the term refers to transactions, which take place completely through the web. When you search for an item on sites such as eBay or Amazon and then pay with a credit card or online checking account, you're conducting the kind of e-commerce that most people think of when the term comes up. That wasn't made possible until the average person began to use the Internet in the 1990's.

Two things happened in the mid-1990's to make this kind of e-commerce a possibility. First, computer security was strengthened enough to make consumers and businesses feel comfortable with conducting these types of transactions online. Second, the average person began to gain familiarity with the web and started using it for everyday activities such as online shopping. Combined with the fact that web design was improving and the speed of the Internet was increasing, e-commerce had a platform for development. In 1995, Amazon.com was launched and we really started seeing the type of e-commerce that we're used to today.

Despite the fact that the web looked a lot then like it does now, there were several factors that inhibited the growth of the online business at this time. For one thing, many people still didn't have high speed Internet in their homes so online shopping tended to be limited to what could be done in the workplace. Additionally, many small businesses invested too much money in creating a web presence and they weren't able to sustain that development due to lack of funds. At the turn of the twenty first century, the dot-com bust happened and many of these businesses went broke.

Of course, we survived the dot-com bust and the Internet came back in a bigger and better way. Today, the average person not only has a home computer but also has the high speed Internet connection that lets him or her move easily between web pages. This makes it easy to do comparison-shopping online. More importantly, the availability of high speed Internet has increased the ability of people to work from home. These people often set up e-commerce sites, which allow them to sell products without needing a whole business behind them. These two factors are combined to make e-commerce become a part of our daily lives. Now if we could only find a way to spend less than we make, we'd all be in good shape.

Words and Expressions

humble	谦卑的
practically	几乎
do billing and invoicing	做票据和发票
toehold	小立足点
familiarity	熟悉度
bust	失败、破产
went broke	破产
survive	幸存

Remark

A Guide to E-mail Writting

建立贸易关系

写作要点：信函简洁清晰，首先陈述从何种渠道了解有关产品的信息，然后介绍自己公司的贸易范围，陈述写信的目的——寻求建立贸易关系，简单陈述合作前景。

Specimen letter

Dear Moyi

We heard from China Council for the Promotion of International Trade that you-KMT are professional manufacturer for high temperature furnace.

We are looking forward to seeking a big co-operation with you and we really want to be your agent in Egypt. So please kindly send us a hard copy for all your products.

Next week we will have an exhibition in Cairo，So please try to send us the catalog and operation manual for the furnace.

We look forward to your early reply.

Best regards，

AHMED ELMASRY

Elmasria for import & export

10 Alekhaa Buildings of Army Corniche Maadi _ kozika- Flat No. 1Cairo- Egypt

Tel：00202 27010104，fax：00202 27000577，mobile：0122222495

点评：这封来自埃及的 e-mail 信函很简洁，首先指出信息的来源，然后表达了希望成为 KMT 产品在埃及代理的意愿。

China Council for the Promotion of International Trade　中国国际贸易促进委员会

Remark

Unit 3 Typical Business Models in Doing E-commerce

Warming-up Questions:

    1. How much do you know about e-commerce business models?

    2. Have you shopped online before? If yes, what was your experience? If no, what do you expect it would be?

Related links:

    1. http://www.kbb.com

    2. http://www.whitehall-inn.com

Although you may think that e-commerce means online stores selling products to consumers on the Web, business-to-business e-commerce dwarfs the consumer side. In this section you will learn how the Web has affected all kinds of online commerce, from business to consumers to governments. First we will explore some e-commerce acronyms.

E-commerce Models

Symbol	Explanation	Example
B2C	Business-to-consumer	Buy tax preparation software and download from the Internet
B2B	Business-to-business	Post REQ (request for quotation) in eMarketplace
C2C	Consumer-to-consumer	Sell old 35mm camera through online auction
G2C	Government-to-consumer	Download a tax form from the IRS site

B2C: Business-to-Consumer

Business-to-consumer (B2C) sales represent the traditional type of e-commerce marketplace in which an online company provides a product to an end consumer. The product might be delivered over the Internet (such as an electronic greeting card, your SAT scores, or downloaded software and music) or shipped from a distribution center to the customer. Package delivery companies such as UPS and FedEX have played an important role in this kind of e-commerce by completing the

Remark

transaction in an efficient manner. Products may be goods or services, including information.

B2B: Business-to-Business

In the B2B e-commerce model, businesses work with other businesses through the Internet. B2B e-commerce marketplaces provide ways to bring buyers and sellers together. These transactions include buying, selling, trading, sales promotion and research. But there is more than purchasing. It's evolved to encompass supply chain management as more companies outsource parts of their supply chain to their trading partners. The relationships between these businesses can be that of vendor, supplier, customer or competitor.

C2C: Consumer-to-Consumer

Online auction sites have enabled users to sell items they no longer need on the Web. Auction sites such as eBay and Yahoo make it easy to list products for sale. To pay for goods, customers can send a money order or personal check to the seller, but these must travel through the mail, delaying the completion of the transaction. New payment services like PayPal and BidPay are intermediary sites that permit sellers to receive payment from auction winners directly through the Internet without the seller having to establish a merchant account for credit card processing.

G2C: Government-to-Consumer

Government sites provide all sorts of helpful information to consumers and businesses. For example, when you are preparing your income tax returns, you can download printable forms from the IRS Web site, or search through the documentation library for information about a tax question. You can even file important forms over the Web. The FAFSA (Free Application for Federal Student Aid) form can be filed electronically by answering questions on the Web.

Online Auctions

Auctions help to determine the price of goods and services for which there is no predetermined price. An online auction is a straightforward yet revolutionary business concept. It brings traditional auctions to the Web by providing services to a differently located customer base and thus increases significantly the opportunity of

Remark

goods and services auctions. Auctions bring the buyers and sellers together in a virtual market.

Online auction companies allow users to include a description (also photo) of a product or service and a bid price to be auctioned for a limited time on their virtual auction sites. No inventories, delivery services, or money transactions (except for the posting fee) are involved in this service. For these reasons, this business model offers enormous profits for leading auctioneers. eBay, Inc. is a good example of a successful auction site.

Online auctions are the fastest growing area of e-commerce. The following features contribute to the popularity of online auctions:

- The auctioneer collects fees from both sellers and buyers.
- The auctioneer sells advertisement on the site.
- Everything (as long as it is legal) can be auctioned.
- The "virtual" audience is all around the world, providing an unprecedented customer base.

Words and Expressions

dwarf *vt.*	使相形下显得矮小或渺小
acronym *n.*	首字母缩略词
quotation *n.*	a price, esp. that will be charged for doing a piece of work 报价
auction *n.*	拍卖
IRS	Internal Revenue Service 国内税务局（美国国内税务局）
register *v.*	登记，注册
symbol *n.*	符号
indicate *vt.*	标示，表明
copyright *n.*	版权
exclusive *adj.*	limited to only one person or group of people 专用的
download *v.*	下载
vendor *n.*	seller 小贩，卖主
virtual *adj.*	虚拟的
bid *n.*	a bid is an offer of a particular amounts of money for something which is for sale 出价
inventory *n.*	a detailed list of all the items in a place 存货清单

Notes

1. **eBay**：eBay 公司成立于 1995 年 9 月，目前是全球最大的网络交易平台之一，为个人用户和企业用户提供国际化的网络交易平台。eBay. com 是一个基于互联网的社区，买家和卖家在一起浏览、买卖商品，eBay 交易平台完全自动化，按

Remark

照类别提供拍卖服务，让卖家罗列出售的东西，买家对感兴趣的东西提出报价。eBay 还有定价拍卖模式，买家和卖家按照卖家确立的固定价格进行交易。

2. **UPS**：United Parcel Service 联合包裹服务公司，目前被广泛地用于电子商务的投递服务。

3. **FedEx**：联邦快递公司。

Exercises

Reading Comprehension

According to the text，answer the following questions.

1. What type of e-commerce does FedEx implement? B2B, B2C or C2C?
2. What are the benefits of B2C e-commerce in your own words?
3. What kind of company is eBay?
4. What are the advantages and disadvantages of C2C online auctions?
5. What does online auction mean?

Translation

A. Translate the following sentences into Chinese.

1. Although you may think that e-commerce means online stores selling products to consumers on the Web, business-to-business e-commerce dwarfs the consumer side.

2. Package delivery companies such as UPS and FedEX have played an important role in this kind of e-commerce by completing the transaction in an efficient manner.

3. To pay for goods, customers can send a money order or personal check to the seller，but these must travel through the mail，delaying the completion of the transaction.

4. Auctions help to determine the price of goods and services for which there is no predetermined price.

5. Online auction companies allow users to include a description（also photo）of a product or service and a bid price to be auctioned for a limited time on their virtual auction sites.

B. Translate the following sentences into English with the given words.

1. 网络影响了人们生活的方方面面，电子商务的出现就是很好的例子。（affect）

2. 网络可以提供我们所需要的各种各样的信息。（provide... for...）

3. 对于现代社会来说，电子商务不再是一个陌生的名词了。（no longer）

4. 网络基础设施的完善是电子商务迅速发展的原因之一。（contribute）

Remark

5. 这个电脑你想用多久就用多久。(as long as)

Supplementary Reading

China Market: B2B E-commerce Valued at Nearly 1.1 Billion Yuan in 1Q08

Press release, May 6; Adam Hwang, DIGITIMES [Tuesday 6 May 2008]

Business-to-business (B2B) e-commerce generated a total transaction value of 1.058 billion yuan (US$148 million) during the first quarter of 2008, slipping by 4.4% on quarter but rising by 19.0% on year, according to China-based consulting company Analysys International.

Of the transaction value, 621 million yuan or 58.7% was due to imports and exports while th remaining 437 million yuan or 41.3% was from domestic trades, Analysys noted.

Business-to-customer (B2C) sales transactions for online shopping during the first quarter reached an estimated total value of 1.282 billion yuan, decreasing by 1.2% on quarter but increasing by 25.7% on year, according to the research firm.

China market: Market share breakdown of leading web portals of B2B services by transaction value, 1Q08

Company	Market share
Alibaba (Chinese)	54.3%
Global Sources	8.7%
Made-in-China (Chinese)	8.1%
HC360 (Chinese)	3.4%
EmedChina (Chinese)	2.6%
MainOne (Chinese)	2.6%
315.com.cn (Chinese)	2.6%
Toocle (Chinese)	2.1%

Source: Analysys International, compiled by Digitimes, May 2008

China market: Market share breakdown of top B2C web portals by total sales transaction value, 1Q08

Company	Market share
DangDang	16.0%
360buy	15.4%
Joyo (Amazon in China)	14.7%
139shop	10.5%
Cncard1	5.5%
NewEgg	3.5%
RedBaby	2.6%
M18	2.5%
7cv	1.6%
China-pub	1.5%
99read	1.2%

Source: Analysys International, compiled by Digitimes, May 2008

A guide to E-mail writting

订单（purchase order）

写作要点：在经过一番询价、讨价之后，询价方通常会向供货方提供一份正式订单，其作用视同供货合同，供应方根据订单的内容进入供货操作流程。下面的例子是美国 MTI 公司给中国 KMT 公司的一份表格式订单。

PURCHASE ORDER

Supplier：KMT Corp Hefei Kejing Materials Tech. Co. Ltd. PO Box 1125 Hefei，Anhui，230031，China **Tel**：86-551-559-1559； **Fax**：86-551-559-2689			**PO#**	KMT-DualZone-100907M
			Purchase Date	10/09/2007
			Date Required	ASAP
			Ship Via	By ocean
			Payment Term	Net 60 days
			Atten.	Mr. Kong

Item#	P/N	Description	Qty.	Unit，USD	Ext. USD
1	OTF-1200X2	OTF-1200X2 Dual Zones Tube Furnace(2″)，OD：50 mm	2	2200 USD	
Total Amount：					4400 USD

Issued by：Mel Jiang	**Signature**：	**Date**：10/09/2007
Ship & Bill to： **MTI Corp.** **2700 Rydin Road，Unit D** **Richmond，CA 94804**	**Please confirm this order as soon as possible. Thanks**	

Notice：Please provide limited warranty for the product（s）we ordered. MTI Corp. reserves the right to return any defective product caused by supplier.

点评：表格化订单的特点是清晰、一目了然。通常用于长期交往的贸易伙伴之间进行定型产品的订货，从而简化了过多的文字描述。Notice 中的提示是对本公司权利自我保护的常用书面语，请认真读懂，甚至熟记。

Remark

Unit 4　E-commerce Success Stories

Warming-up questions:

1. What factors can be attributed to the success of eBay?
2. What is the business model of eBay?

Related Links:

1. http: //wwp. greenwichmeantime. com/time-zone/usa/websites/ebay. com/
2. http: //global. ebay. com/gbh/home? keyword=ebay&crlp=728694338 _ 11194

eBay — The World's Largest Auction Site

eBay is one of the most profitable e-business. The successful online auction house has its roots in a 50-year-old novelty item—Pez candy dispensers. Pam Omidyar, an avid collector of Pez candy dispenser, came up with the idea of trading them over the Internet. When she expressed this idea to her boyfriend (now her husband), Pierre Omidyar, he was instantly struck with the soon-to-be-famous e-business auction concept.

• The Solution

In 1995, the Omidyars created a company called AuctionWeb. The company was renamed eBay and had since become the premier online auction house, with millions of unique auctions in progress and over 500000 new items added each day. Today, eBay is much more than an auction house, but its initial success was in electronic auctions.

The initial business model of eBay was to provide an electronic infrastructure for conducting mostly C2C auctions. There is no auctioneer; technology manages the auctioning process.

On eBay, people can buy and sell just about anything. The company collects a submission fee upfront, plus a commission as a percentage of the sale amount. The submission fee is based on the amount of exposure the seller wants their item to receive, with a higher fee if the seller would like the item to be among the featured auctions in a specific product category, and an even higher fee if they want the item to be listed on the eBay home page under Featured Items. Another attention-grab-

Remark

bing option is to publish the product listing in a boldface font (for an additional charge).

The auction process begins when the seller fills in the appropriate registration information and posts a description of the item for sale. The seller must specify a minimum opening bid. If potential buyers feel this price is too high, the item may not receive any bids. Sellers might set the opening bid lower than the reserve price, a minimum acceptable bid price, to generate bidding activity.

If a successful bid is made, the seller and the buyer negotiate the payment method, shipping details, warranty, and other particulars. eBay serves as a liaison between the parties; it is the interface through which sellers and buyers can conduct business. eBay does not maintain a costly physical inventory or deal with shipping, handling, or other services that businesses such as Amazon. com and other retailers must provide. The eBay site basically serves individuals, but it also caters to small businesses.

In 2001, eBay started to auction fine art in collaboration with *icollector. com* of the United Kingdom and with the art auction house Sotheby's (*sothebys. com*), whose auction page is on eBay's main menu. Due to lack of profit, as of May 2003, eBay and Sotheby's discontinued separate online auctions and began placing emphasis on promoting Sotheby's live auction through eBay's Live Auctions technology while they also continue to build eBay's highly successful arts and antiques categories. The Sothebys. com Web site still exists, but now is focused on supporting Sotheby's live auction business.

In addition, eBay operates globally, permitting international trades to take place. Country-specific sites are located in over 25 countries, including the United States, Canada, France, Sweden, Brazil, the United Kingdom, Australia, Singapore, and Japan. Buyers from more than 150 other countries participate. eBay also operates a business exchange in which SMEs can buy and sell new and used merchandise in B2B or B2C modes.

eBay has over 60 local sites in the United States that enable users to easily find items located near them, to browse through items of local interest, and to meet face-to-face to conclude transactions. In addition, some eBay sites, such as eBay Motors, concentrate on specialty items. Trading can be done from anywhere, at any time. Wireless trading is also possible.

In 2002, eBay Seller Payment Protection began making it safer to sell on eBay. Now sellers are protected against bad checks and fraudulent credit card purchases. The service offers credit card chargeback protection, guaranteed electronic checks secure processing, and privacy protection. After a few years of successful operation and tens of million of loyal members, eBay decided to leverage its large

Remark

(

customer base and started to do e-tailing, mostly at fixed prices. This may have been in response to Amazon. com's decision to start auctions or it may have been a logical idea for a diversification. By 2003, eBay operated several specialty sites.

In addition to eBay Motors cited earlier, *half. com*, the famous discount e-tailer, is now part of eBay, and so is *PayPal. com*, the P2P payment company. A special feature is eBay Stores. These stores are rented to individuals and companies. The renting companies can use these stores to sell catalogs of conduct auctions. In 2002, eBay introduced the Business Marketplace, located at *ebaybusiness. com*. This site brings together all business-related listings on eBay into one destination, making it easier for small businesses to find the equipment and supplies they need.

• The Results

The impact of eBay on e-business has been profound. Its founders took a limited-access off-line business model and, by using the Internet, were able to bring it to the desktops of consumers worldwide. This business model consistently generates a profit and promotes a sense of community—a near addiction that keeps traders coming back.

eBay is the world's largest auction site, with a community of close to 50 million registered users as of fall 2002. According to company financial statements, in 2002, it transacted over $14. 7 billion in sales.

Why Can eBay Get Success?

Perhaps we can get the answer from the following speech.

The speech of Pierre Omidyar (Posted: February 26, 1996, To: eBay Community)

I launched eBay's AuctionWeb on Labor Day, 1995. Since then, the site has become more popular than I ever expected, and I began to realize that this was indeed a grand experiment in Internet commerce. By creating an open market that encourages honest dealings, I hope to make it easier to conduct business with strangers over the net.

Most people are honest. And they mean well. Some people go out of their way to make things right. I've heard great stories about the honesty of people here. But some people are dishonest. Or deceptive. This is true here, in the newsgroups, in the classifieds, and right next door. It's a fact of life. But here, those people can't hide. We'll drive them away. Protect others from them. This grand hope depends on your active participation. Become a registered user. Use our feedback forum. Give praise where it is due; make complaints where appropriate. For the past

Remark

six months, I've been developing this system single-handedly, in my spare time. Along the way, I've dealt with complaints among participants. But those complaints have amounted to only a handful. We've had close to 10,000 auctions since opening. And only a few dozen complaints.

Now, we have an open forum. Use it. Make your complaints in the open. Better yet, give your praise in the open. Let everyone know what a joy it was to deal with someone. Above all, conduct yourself in a professional manner. Deal with others the way you would have them deal with you. Remember that you are usually dealing with individuals, just like yourself. Subject to making mistakes. Well-meaning, but wrong on occasion. That's just human. We can live with that. We can deal with that. We can still make deals with that. Thanks for participating. Good luck, and good business!

Regards,

Pierre Omidyar

Let us end the unit with the words of Prof. Ben Gomes-Casseres "*eBay has both streamlined and globalized traditional person-to-person trading, which has traditionally been conducted through such forms as garage sales, collectibles shows, flea markets and more, with their web interface*".

eBay gets success, that is because eBay selects a great business concept—eBay is a company that's in the business of connecting people, not selling them things.

Words and expressions

profitable *adj.*	producing a profit or a useful result	有利可图的，可赚钱的
dispenser *n.*	药剂师；自动售货机	
novelty *n.*	新奇的东西，小商品	
avid *adj.*	doing something as much as possible	热心的，渴望的
instantly *adv.*	immediately 立即地，即刻地	
premier *adj.*	best or most important 最早的，首要的	
infrastructure *n.*	基础结构、设施	
upfront *adj.*	预付的	
liaison *n.*	联系	
fraudulent *adj.*	欺诈的，欺骗的	
leverage *v.*	影响；杠杆作用	
diversification *n.*	多样化	
deceptive *adj.*	欺骗的	
addiction *n.*	上瘾	
cite *vt.*	引用，举出	
profound *adj.*	深远的	

Remark

launch *vt.*   开办，发动，发起

amount to   总计，等于

cater to   迎合；为……服务

subject to   易受……的，易遭受……的

Notes

1. **Pez candy dispensers**   一种糖果罐子，eBay 是一个为了收集糖果罐创立的网站。1995 年，Pierre Omidyar 和他的未婚妻 Pam Wesley 从波斯顿搬家到了硅谷。当时 Pierre 的妻子是一个收集 PEZ dispensers（一种糖果罐子）的爱好者，但是在硅谷找不到其他的收藏者，Pierre 觉得也许互联网会是个好主意，就专门架设了 AuctionWeb.com 网站（eBay 的前身），号召各路 Pez dispensers 的收集者把他们的收藏品拿到网上来拍卖。后来他组建了一个咨询公司，取名 "EchoBay 技术公司"，转而用 eBay.com 注册。

2. **boldface font**   黑体字

3. **SME**   Small and Medium Enterprises   中小企业

Exercises

Reading Comprehension

According to the text，answer the following questions.

1. What is eBay's initial business model?

2. How does a buyer conduct an auction on eBay?

3. What methods have been adopted to protect sellers against bad checks and fraudulent credit card purchases?

4. According to Pierre Omidyar，what is highly appreciated in doing business online?

5. What does "ebay is a company that's in the business of connecting people, not selling them things" mean?

Translation

A. Translate the following sentences into Chinese.

1. If a successful bid is made，the seller and the buyer negotiate the payment method，shipping details，warranty，and other particulars.

2. eBay does not maintain a costly physical inventory or deal with shipping, handling，or other services that businesses such as *Amazon.com* and other retailers must provide.

3. After a few years of successful operation and tens of million of loyal members，eBay decided to leverage its large customer base and started to do e-tailing,

Remark

mostly at fixed prices.

4. This site brings together all business-related listings on eBay into one destination, making it easier for small businesses to find the equipment and supplies they need.

5. eBay has both streamlined and globalized traditional person-to-person trading, which has traditionally been conducted through such forms as garage sales, collectibles shows, flea markets and more, with their web interface.

B. Translate the following sentences into English.

1. 网上购物的方式适合年轻人的口味。(cater to)

2. 货币的升值或贬值很容易受到外界因素的影响。(subject to)

3. 这种手段无异于是欺诈。(amount to)

Supplementary Reading

Factors to the Success of E-commerce

Several factors have a role in the success of any e-commerce venture. They may include:

1. Providing value to customers. Vendors can achieve this by offering a product or product-line that attracts potential customers at a competitive price, as in non-electronic commerce.

2. Providing service and performance. Offering a responsive, user-friendly purchasing experience, just like a flesh-and-blood retailer, may go some way to achieving these goals.

3. Providing an attractive website. The tasteful use of colour, graphics, animation, photographs, fonts, and white-space percentage may aid success in this respect.

4. Providing an incentive for customers to buy and to return. Sales promotions to this end can involve coupons, special offers, and discounts. Cross-linked websites and advertising affiliate programs can also help.

5. Providing personal attention. Personalized web sites, purchase suggestions, and personalized special offers may go some of the way to substituting for the face-to-face human interaction found at a traditional point of sale.

6. Providing a sense of community. Chat rooms, discussion boards, soliciting customer input, loyalty schemes and affinity programs can help in this respect.

7. Providing reliability and security. Parallel servers, hardware redundancy, fail-safe technology, information encryption, and firewalls can enhance this requirement.

8. Providing a 360-degree view of the customer relationship, defined as ensuring that all employees, suppliers, and partners have a complete view, and the

Remark

same view, of the customer. However, customers may not appreciate the big brother experience.

9. Owning the customer's total experience. E-tailers foster this by treating any contacts with a customer as part of a total experience, an experience that becomes synonymous with the brand.

10. Streamlining business processes, possibly through re-engineering and information technologies.

11. Letting customers help themselves. Provision of a self-serve site, easy to use without assistance, can help in this respect.

12. Helping customers do their job of consuming. E-tailers can provide such help through ample comparative information and good search facilities. Provision of component information and safety-and-health comments may assist e-tailers to define the customers' job.

13. Constructing a commercially sound business model. If this key success factor had appeared in textbooks in 2000, many of the dot. coms might not have gone bust.

14. Engineering an electronic value chain in which one focuses on a "limited" number of core competencies — the opposite of a one-stop shop. (Electronic stores can appear either specialist or generalist if properly programmed.)

15. Operating on or near the cutting edge of technology and staying there as technology changes (but remembering that the fundamentals of commerce remain indifferent to technology).

16. Setting up an organization of sufficient alertness and agility to respond quickly to any changes in the economic, social and physical environment.

Words and Expressions

vendor	*n.*	小贩
responsive	*adj.*	立刻有反应的
animation	*n.*	动画
incentive	*n.*	动机
coupons	*n.*	折价券
affiliate	*v.*	参加、使加入
solicit	*v.*	请求、恳求
affinity	*n.*	密切的关系
redundancy	*n.*	冗余
fail-safe	*adj.*	不出错的
synonymous	*adj.*	近义的
Streamline	*v.*	使合理化、效率化
agility	*n.*	灵活性

A Guide to E-mail writting

通　告

写作要点：语言规范、严谨，条理清晰，对所公告的事件描述准确，采取的措施以及产生后果简要陈述。

Specimen letter

eBay International AG sent this message.

NOTICE：eBay Registration Suspension-Shill Bidding

Hello,

This email is to notify you that your account has been suspended for a minimum of 7 days due to violation of our Shill Bidding Policy.

Shill Bidding is bidding that artificially increases an item's price or apparent desirability. Shill Bidding is prohibited on eBay. Information on eBay's Shill Bidding Policy can be found at:

http：//pages. ebay. com/help/policies/seller-shill-bidding. html

Your account has been found to be involved in Shill Bidding with the following associated accounts：naw017，2ndrew，drachel，gress，5john，gfeen，doco，6roco，naw0103.

You are prohibited from using eBay in any way (including use of other existing accounts or registering new accounts) during your suspension.

Any auctions you currently have open have been cancelled. Please note that any fees incurred for these auctions will not be credited back to your account.

Your account will remain suspended for a minimum of 7 days，after which time you may appeal the suspension by replying to this email.

If you want to unsuspend your account now click the link below：

http：//signin. ebay. com/ws/eBayISAPI. dll？SignIn&Unsuspend

Regards,

SafeHarbor Department

eBay，Inc.

点评：这是由 eBay 公司开给 MTI 公司的暂时吊销经营资格的通知单。吊销的理由是违反了 Shill-bidding Policy：拍卖过程中的"托"出价条款。吊销时间为 7 天，在此期间不得使用任何其他 eBay 账号进行任何经营活动。这类信函的特点是清晰明了、直奔主题，有点接近法律文书，十分严谨。

Unit 5　The Internet and the World Wide Web

Warming-up Questions:

1. What is the difference between the Internet and World Wide Web?
2. Do you know how to make purchases on the Internet? Give an example.
3. What is the relationship between the Internet and e-commerce?

Related Links:

1. http://www. elsop. com/wrc/h . web. htm
2. http://www. webopedia. com/DidYouKnow/Internet/2002/Web _ vs _ Internet. asp

The Internet

The Internet, a group of worldwide information highways and resources, is enabling the world to truly become an information society. Its origins can be traced to an experimental network established with funding from the Advanced Research Project Agency (ARPA) of the US Department of Defense (DoD), to enable the scientists engaged on DoD projects to communicate with one another. Electronic mail over the ARPAnet, as it was called, was a great success. The National Science Foundation (NSF) took over the academic community network project in the mid-1980's, after defense traffic was moved away from the ARPAnet to MILNET. In 1987, the NSF created NSFnet.

NSF upgraded the lines to 56 Kbps to connect the five supercomputer centers. Regional and corporate networks were permitted to connect to NSFnet. Geographically contiguous chains were created by connecting networks to their nearest neighbors. Each chain was connected to a supercomputer center. This enabled any computer on any network to communicate with any other network computer by using the store and forward techniques. It is the NSFnet, which was later christened as the Internet.

The Internet has continued to grow ever since. Today, the Internet has two types of backbone: NSFnet and commercial Internet. The US federal government which owns the NSFnet forbids its commercial use. The commercial Internet, on

Remark

the other hand, comprises several private backbones run by a number of Internet Service Providers (ISPs). The users have to pay for Internet services for access through these routes. One such private backbone is operated by Advanced Network & Services Inc. (ANS), owned by IBM, MCI, and Merit Inc. It was only in 1991 that a set of small commercial networks created the Commercial Internet Exchange (CIX) for commercial use.

The Internet is neither run nor owned by anyone. Every organization that is plugged into the Internet is responsible for its own computers. It is more or less an anarchy. Among its advantages are: no membership fees, nor censorship, no government control. The prominent disadvantage is that when something goes wrong, there is no central control to ask for help. However, a number of Internet Technical Groups coordinate the Internet's basic working.

The World Wide Web

The World Wide Web (WWW) or the Web is a system for organizing, linking, and providing point-and-click access among related Internet files, resources, and services. The point-and-click access is due to the underlying hypertext or hypermedia approach of the Web search engine. The Web is an Internet—based navigational system, an information distribution or management system with tremendous potential for commerce, which has just begun to be exploited. The Web has become an integral part of the Internet.

Just like the Internet itself, the World Wide Web has grown in an anarchic manner. No person, company, or organization owns the Web. It is a distributed system with millions of users, and perhaps an equal number of Web authors, who contribute to this electronic warehouse. The applications of this global database range from education to entertainment to government to commerce. Websites are hosted by educational, commercial, and government institutions. According to the statistics available by Anonymous FTP from nic. merit. edu. , the Web traffic comprises the following: US educational—49%, US commercial—20%, US government—9%, other countries—22%.

The Web has indeed graduated into an enabling mechanism for Electronic Commerce.

Differences Between the Internet and World Wide Web

Many people use the terms Internet and World Wide Web interchangeably, but in fact the two terms are not synonymous. The Internet and the Web are two

Remark

separate but related things.

The Internet is a massive network of networks, a networking infrastructure. It connects millions of computers together globally, forming a network in which any computer can communicate with any other computer as long as they are both connected to the Internet. Information that travels over the Internet does so via a variety of languages known as protocols.

The World Wide Web, or simply Web, is a way of accessing information over the medium of the Internet. It is an information-sharing model that is built on top of the Internet. The Web uses the HTTP protocol, only one of the languages spoken over the Internet, to transmit data. Web services, which use HTTP to allow applications to communicate in order to exchange business logic, use the Web to share information. The Web also utilizes browsers, such as Internet Explorer or Netscape, to access Web documents called Web pages that are linked to each other via hyperlinks. Web documents also contain graphics, sounds, text and video.

The Web is just one of the ways that information can be disseminated over the Internet. The Internet, not the Web, is also used for E-mail, which relies on SMTP, Usenet news groups, instant messaging and FTP. So the Web is just a portion of the Internet, albeit a large portion, but the two terms are not synonymous and should not be confused.

The Web and E-commerce

With the World Wide Web in the homes and businesses of tens of millions of people worldwide, businesses now have a new and exciting method of conveying their corporate messages. Forward-thinking companies were quick to take advantage of the unique advantages that the World Wide Web presented. They began to shift resources away from traditional advertising methods into Web campaigns. Here was a totally revolutionary way to achieve a level of interactivity and intimacy with consumers that marketers had never before dreamed possible. Instead of trying to capture the attention of potential consumers as with radio, television, and newspaper advertisements, here was a system in which consumers were actually seeking out product and service information. Companies no longer had to sit and hope that consumers would follow an advertisement to the store. They could now present corporate information to consumers at the point of sale. Consumers exposed to an advertisement could immediately make a purchase. Fortune 500 companies quickly began to compile Web budgets; most were spending between $ 840,000 to $ 1.5 million just to get their Web sites up and running. Many Fortune 500 companies continue to spend as much as several hundred thousand dollars per year to

Remark

maintain and market their Web sites (Internet World, 1996).

As the Web continued to grow, Web sites became more than just online brochures. Companies quickly began to build not only sites with appealing graphic content and informative copy, but sites that implemented secured credit systems to accept online purchases and integrated entire database to compile consumer information and manage products online. The new point-of-purchase situation that was created with the Web enabled sellers to generate revenue from additional sources. Manufactures could sell directly to consumers, smaller domestic companies could sell internationally, and entire niches of new businesses began to pop up almost daily. This new method of E-commerce quickly made the Web become an even more powerful business resource.

However, with this new way to shop for products came new challenges for businesses. First and foremost, how were consumers going to pay for their purchases? Second, given experiences with individuals gaining uninvited access to computer networks security issues emerged as it became apparent that large amounts of money would be changing hands daily over the new networks. Finally, businesses needed to address the subtle challenges of E-commerce, such as the need for new methods of organizing products online and for maximizing consumer convenience, as well as for completely new marketing strategies and techniques.

Words and Expressions

funding *n.*		资金，基金，专款
disperse *v.*		（使某人/某物）散开；分散
academic *adj.*	of theoretical interest only	学术的
traffic *n.*		通信量
corporate *adj.*		团体的，共同的；社团的
contiguous *adj.*	touching; neighbouring; near	邻近的，连接的，相邻的
christen *v.*	give a name to	命名为
backbone *n.*		中枢链路；供给中心
anarchy *n.*		无政府状态
prominent *adj.*	easily seen; conspicuous	显著的，突出的
navigational *adj.*	of or relating to navigation	导航的，指导的
integral *adj.*	necessary for completeness	构成整体所必需的，必不可少的，完整的
anarchic *adj.*	without law or control	无政府状态的，无法无天的
interchangeably *adv.*	in an interchangeable manner	可交换地
synonymous *adj.*	meaning the same or nearly the same	同义的
infrastructure *n.*		基础设施，基础结构

Remark

protocol *n.*	rules determining the format and transmission of data　草案，协议
disseminate *v.*	cause to become widely known　散播，传播，宣传
albeit *conj.*	虽然
convey *v.*	输送
intimacy *n.*	close or warm friendship　熟悉，亲密，密切关系
capture *v.*	抓取，获得，迷住
compile *v.*	编译
informative *adj.*	提供大量资料或信息
emerge *v.*	become known　暴露，知悉，显现，显露；come out or up　出现
trace sb. /sth. to sth.	追踪，追溯，探索，跟踪
take over	接手，接替，接任
plug into	把插头插入，接通
be responsible for	担负（对……负责）
base on	基于，作为……的基础
in addition to	除……之外（还）
in turn	依次，轮流
contribute to	有助于，贡献给
range from... to	在……和……之间变动
rely on	依靠，信赖
take advantage of	利用
shift... away	移走
seek out	寻出，挑出
pop up	突然出现，冒出来
first and foremost	首先，第一

Notes

1. ARPA（Advanced Research Projects Agency）：（美国国防部）高级研究计划署

2. NSF（National Science Foundation）：国家科学基金

3. Kbps（Kilo-Bytes Per Second）：每秒千字节；千字节/秒

4. IBM（International Business Machine）：（美国）国际商用机器公司

5. MCI（Media Control Internet）：媒体控制接口（美国著名的通信公司）

6. Mbps（Mega Bites Per Second）：兆位/秒

7. SP（Internet Service Provider）：因特网服务提供者

8. CIX（Commercial Internet Exchange）：Internet 商业交流

Remark

Exercises

Reading Comprehension

According to the text，answer the following questions.

1. What makes any computer on any network to communicate with any other network computer by using the store and forward techniques?

2. Why do we say the Internet is more or less an anarchy?

3. What enables an Internet user to access many services and resources on the Internet?

4. As the Web continued to grow，what sites do companies quickly begin to build ? What for?

5. What new challenges for business came with the new way to shop for products?

Translation

A. Translate the following sentences into Chinese.

1. The Internet is neither run nor owned by anyone. Every organization that is plugged into the Internet is responsible for its own computers.

2. It was only in 1991 that a set of small commercial networks created the Commercial Internet Exchange (CIX) for commercial use.

3. The World Wide Web (WWW) or the Web is a system for organizing, linking, and providing point-and-click access among related Internet files, resources, and services.

4. Many people use the terms Internet and World Wide Web interchangeably, but in fact the two terms are not synonymous. The Internet and the Web are two separate but related things.

5. Companies no longer had to sit and hope that consumers would follow an advertisement to the store. They could now present corporate information to consumers at the point of sale.

B. Translate the following sentences into English with the given words or expressions.

1. 该公司已被美国一企业集团接管。(take over)

2. 她已被提升为销售部主任。(upgrade sb. /sth. to sb. /sth.)

3. 他们充分利用网络资源。(take advantage of)

4. 我们怎样才能在信息的海洋中找出我们所需要的信息？(seek out)

5. 当我们打开某一个网页的时候，广告立刻跳出来了。(pop up)

Supplementary Reading

Common Security Vulnerabilities in E-commerce Systems

The remarkable increase in online transactions has been accompanied by an e-

Remark

qual rise in the

number and type of attacks against the security of online payment systems. The security vulnerabilities in e-commerce systems come in different ways. The following sections look at common security vulnerabilities that have been discovered in shopping cart and online payment systems.

SQL Injection

SQL injection refers to the insertion of SQL meta-characters in user input, such that the attacker's queries are executed by the back-end database. Typically, attackers will first determine if a site is vulnerable to such an attack by sending in the single-quote (') character. The results from an SQL injection attack on a vulnerable site may range from a detailed error message, which discloses the back-end technology being used, or allowing the attacker to access restricted areas of the site because he manipulated the query to an always-true Boolean value, or it may even allow the execution of operating system commands.

Price Manipulation

This is a vulnerability that is almost completely unique to online shopping carts and payment gateways. In the most common occurrence of this vulnerability, the total payable price of the purchased goods is stored in a hidden HTML field of a dynamically generated web page. An attacker can use a web application proxy such as Achilles [ref 5] to simply modify the amount that is payable, when this information flows from the user's browser to the web server.

Remote command execution

The most devastating web application vulnerabilities occur when the CGI script allows an attacker to execute operating system commands due to inadequate input validation. This is most common with the use of the 'system' call in Perl and PHP scripts. Using a command separator and other shell metacharacters, it is possible for the attacker to execute commands with the privileges of the web server.

Countermeasures

The most important point is to build security into the web application at the design stage itself. In fact, one of the key activities during the design phase should be a detailed risk assessment exercise. Here, the team must identify the key information assets that the web application will be dealing with. These could include configuration information, user transaction details, session IDs, credit card numbers, etc. Each of these information assets needs to be classified in terms of sensitivity. Depending on the tentative architecture chosen, the developers along with security experts must analyze the threats, impact, vulnerabilities and threat probabilities for the system. Once these risks are listed out, system countermeasures must be designed and if necessary the architecture itself may be modified. Countermeasures should also include strict input validation routines, a 3-tier modular architecture, use of open-source cryptographic standards, and other secure coding practices.

Notes

SQL 全称是"结构化查询语言（Structured Query Language）"，最早的是 IBM 的圣约瑟研究实验室为其关系数据库管理系统 SYSTEM R 开发的一种查询语言，它的前身是 SQUARE 语言。

Words and Expressions

remarkable *adj.*		显著的
vulnerability *n.*		弱点、易受攻击处
manipulate *v.*		操纵
proxy *n.*		代理人（权）
validation *n.*		合法化
configuration *n.*		配置、外型
cryptographic *n.*		密码法

A Guide to E-mail Writting

询价（enquiry）

写作要点：询价是对所要订购的产品的价格和参数进行问询。要开门见山地指出写信的目的，对问询的产品描述一定要做到准确翔实，以便供应方掌握可靠的信息资源，提供准确的报价。

Specimen Letter

Dear Sir/Madam,

We are looking for the following substrates：

(100),(111) LSAT substrates, prime quality, 1 side polished and size 2mm× 0.5mm (preferred).

(100),(110),(111) step/etched Nb-STO substrates, prime quality, 1 side polished and size 15mm×15mm×0.5mm (preferred).

Could you provide me with the size of the substrate, and a quotation of the above substrates by today, 18th March 2008?

I look forward to your reply.

Thank you.

Regards,

Alicia Huang

Institute of Materials Research and Engineering IMRE

3 Research Link

Singapore 11760

点评：询价方是新加坡材料工程学院，出价方是 KMT（中科院合肥科晶公司）。信中引用了大量的技术符号如：LSAT 铝钽酸锶镧，Nb-STO 掺铌的钛酸锶，(100)(111) 是指晶向，1 side polished 是单面抛光的意思等。所使用的语言简明扼要、约定俗成。

Remark

Unit 6   Buying Online

Warming-up Questions:

  1. Do you think buying online makes your life easy?

  2. Can you give at least one reason why people like buying things online?

Related links:

  1. http: //www. calm-sea com/blog/userl/Reading/archives/2006

  2. http: //www. oag. state. ny. us/consumer/tips/online _ buytips. html

• Buying Online

The Internet can teach you to use your computer, help you find a job, download an e-mail program, or book a flight to New York. It can let you buy anything you want, you needn't visit a shop personally. It doesn't matter if you are buying a best-selling book for yourself or sending flowers to a friend. Buying online is quick, easy, and safe if you know what to do.

All kinds of products and services are offered for sale online. In this unit, you will see how to shop online. You'll learn how to locate the retail product you want and how to place your order safely.

Online shopping is one of the more attractive features of the Internet. Parents can peruse their favorite shopping sites after the little children are down for a nap. At any time and any place, consumers can access information via the Internet. Anyone with an Internet connection can buy gourmet food from Beijing, tulips from Holland, tickets to a concert in Shanghai, or clothing from stores in far corners of the world—all from a single location in a few minutes. It doesn't matter where you live or when you shop, as long as you have an Internet connection and a way to pay for the item.

All of the major search engines have shopping sections. Yahoo's shopping link shows ads from retailers as well as links to a number of major categories. Clicking a category link such as DVD and Videos leads to more specific links for that area. You can also conduct a direct search for a product. If shopping for a digital camera, you can either follow links or enter the phrase in the search box.

The Google Web Directory also has many shopping topics within its shopping

Remark

category. You'll see links for everything from Antiques and Collectibles to Wholesale.

Some companies use cookies to keep track of your navigation through the site. By doing this, the company can determine your preferences and even personalize the site for you the next time you visit. For example, an online clothing catalog might note that you are interested in swimming-costume. The next time you visit, the site can retrieve this information about you from cookie and immediately show you its best deals on swimming-costume and swimming-related products, such as swimming-glasses.

Finding the Good Life on the Internet

Have you ever needed to buy flowers in a hurry? You may have forgotten a family birthday, or wanted to send a congratulatory bouquet or express sympathy. If you need to send flowers to someone in another place, you probably don't know the reliable florist's name there. And although you could visit a local florist to look through pictures of arrangements, choose one and arrange for it to be delivered, you can do all of these things with much less difficulty online.

You can use the Internet to locate service providers, too. Lawn care services, plumbers, and rental agencies want you to use their Web sites; In order that you can find them easily, many service providers advertise so.

If you have bought entertainment tickets recently, you know that most of these sales are done electronically through ticket services. You can jump into that role yourself and save money by buying tickets online.

It is not surprising that computer manufacturers make it easy for their buyers to configure systems and buy online. If you want to shop for a car online. Car manufacturers' Web sites will help you understand models and options, but won't sell a car to you. The center shows you how to find the car you want and how much it will cost. The site reminds you that you can't definitively figure the value of a trade-in online, nor can you take a test drive. To actually purchase the car, you will have to go to a dealer.

Making the Purchase

When you complete your shopping and decide what you want to buy, it's time to place the items you have selected into your shopping cart and proceed to the checkout counter. This is what buyers are accustomed to doing in stores, and the same process is repeated for most online purchases. Here, the shopping cart is a

Remark

virtual one that keeps track of the quantity, price, and features of the items you have selected. When you add items to the shopping cart, the site may ask you if you want to keep shopping or proceed to checkout. The site may suggest additional items or accessories to go with what you have chosen. Like a friendly sales clerk, the Web site guides you through the sale.

Once you have filled your shopping cart, it's time to proceed to checkout. It's important to understand the security precautions in place at the site. Unless you are absolutely sure that the information is protected, you won't provide any personal information or your credit card number.

Words and Expressions

retail *v.* & *n.*	to sell in small quantities directly to the ultimate consumer 零售
peruse *v.*	read carefully or thoroughly 读;(尤指)细阅;审阅
nap *n.*	小睡;打盹(尤指在白天)
access *v.*	存取(计算机文件)
via *prep.*	by way of (sth.); through 经由(某事物);通过
gourmet *n.*	美食家
tulip *n.*	郁金香
antique *n.*	古物,古董
collectible *n.*	收藏品
wholesale *n.*	批发
congratulatory	庆祝的,祝贺的
bouquet *n.*	花束
reliable *adj.*	worthy of reliance or trust 可靠的
rental agency	租赁公司
configure *v.*	改变
shopping cart	购物车
checkout counter	付账柜台
virtual *adj.*	实际上的,事实上的
accessory *n.*	a supplementary component that improves capability 附件;附属品
security *n.*	安全
jump into	踊跃或热切地投入(某事)
keep track of	记录;保持联系

Notes

cookie: a cookie is a file of information about you that Web sites create and

Remark

store on your hard drive when you visit the site.

Exercises

Reading Comprehension

According to the text，answer the following questions.

1. According to the text，what can you do with the Internet?

2. When and where can consumers access information via the Internet?

3. How do companies track consumers? Give an example.

4. When you decide what you want to purchase，what will you de next?

5. Why is it important to understand the security precautions in place at the site?

Translation

A. Translate the following sentences into Chinese.

1. Online shopping is one of the more attractive features of the Internet. Parents can peruse their favorite shopping sites after the little children are down for a nap. At any time and any place，consumers can access information via the Internet.

2. You can use the Internet to locate service providers，too. Lawn care services，plumbers，and rental agencies want you to use their Web sites; many advertise so that you can find them easily.

3. It's important to understand the security precautions in place at the site. Unless you are absolutely sure that the information is protected，you won't provide any personal information or your credit card number.

4. If you have bought entertainment tickets recently，you know that most of these sales are done electronically through ticket services.

5. When you complete your shopping and decide what you want to buy，it's time to place the items you have selected into your shopping cart and proceed to the checkout counter. This is what buyers are accustomed to doing in stores，and the same process is repeated for most online purchases.

B. Translate the following sentences into English with the given words or expressions.

1. 对于大多数人来说，网上购物既是方便的又是很快乐的。(as well as)

2. 网络商店会跟踪记录你所买过的产品信息。(keep track of)

3. 当你再次购物的时候，系统会自动检索你先前的记录。(retrieve)

4. 人们很快就习惯了网络购物这种模式。(be accustomed to)

5. 可以改变软件，以防重要信息的泄露。(configure)

Remark

Supplementary Reading

10 Tips for Smart Holiday Shopping Online

Some of us go online to shop to avoid crowds, some to save gas, and some for the convenience of shopping at any time of day or night. Experts are predicting that consumers will spend more online this holiday season than ever. In fact, a recent Forrester study reports that 11 percent of online shoppers said they would do three-quarters or more of their holiday spending online, translating to an estimated $33 billion in 2007, up from $27 billion in 2006.

To reduce the risk of a rip-off—and to protect your personal information and your computer from identity thieves and hackers—the FTC and NCSA offer these tips for safer and smarter online shopping this holiday season:

Check out the seller. If you're thinking about shopping on a site with which you're not familiar, do some independent research before you buy.

Call the seller's phone number;

Type the site's name into a search engine;

Read the site's privacy policy to learn how it uses and shares your personal information;

Consider using a software toolbar that rates websites and warns you if a site has gotten unfavorable reports from experts and other Internet users.

Read return policies. Despite your best intentions, some gifts may need to be returned or exchanged. Before you buy, read the return policy. Some retailers give customers extra time so gifts can be returned or exchanged after the holidays; others give purchasers as little as a week—if they accept returns at all. Find out who covers the shipping cost and if your online purchase can be returned to a brick-and-mortar store.

Know what you're getting. Read the seller's product description closely. Name-brand items at greatly reduced prices could be counterfeit.

Don't fall for a false email or pop-up. Legitimate companies don't send unsolicited email messages asking for your password or login name, or your financial information. But scammers do. In fact, crooks often send emails that look just like they're from legitimate companies—but direct you to click on a link, where they ask for your personal information.

Look for signs a site is safe. When you're ready to buy something from a seller you trust, look for signs that the site is secure—such as a closed padlock on the browser's status bar — before you enter your personal and financial information.

Secure your computer. At a minimum, your computer should have anti-virus and anti-spyware software, and a firewall. Security software must be updated regu-

Remark

larly to help protect against the latest threats.

Consider how you'll pay. Credit cards generally are a safe option because they allow buyers to seek a credit from the issuer if the product isn't delivered or isn't what was ordered. Also, if your credit card number is stolen, you generally won't be liable for more than $50 in charges.

Know the full price, and check out incentives. If you're looking for the best deal, compare total costs, including shipping and handling. The holiday season is prime time for online retailers, and many are offering incentives like free shipping. But some "free" shipping deals may come with strings attached, such as requirements to spend a minimum amount or buy certain products. Consider whether one company offers a more generous return policy.

Keep a paper trail. Print and save records of your online transactions, including the product description and price, the online receipt, and copies of any email you exchange with the seller. Read your credit card statements as soon as you get them to make sure there aren't any unauthorized charges.

Turn your computer off when you're finished shopping. Many people leave their computers running 24/7, the dream scenario for scammers who want to install malicious software on your machine and then control it remotely to commit cyber crime. To be extra safe, switch off your computer when you are not using it.

Notes

1. **FTC** The Federal Trade Commission, the nation's consumer protection agency, and the National

2. **NCSA** Cyber Security Alliance , a non-profit organization devoted to cyber security education and awareness,

Words and expressions

rip-off	偷窃
legitimate *adj.*	合法的
unsolicited *adj.*	非请求的
scammer *n.*	设计诡计的人
crooks *n.*	骗子
padlock *v.*	禁止进入
prime *adj.*	最好的
string *n.*	一串
scenario *n.*	想定的场景
malicious *adj.*	怀恶意的

Remark

A Guide to E-mail Writting

报价（quotation）

写作要点：指明你要回复的是哪封来信，直接给出对方所需要的信息，对产品的描述要准确、清晰，还需要给出相关的一些费用的报价，比如：运费、税等。

Specimen Letter

Dear Alicia

Thank you for your inquiry，I am pleased to quote as follows：

(100)，(111) LSAT substrates，prime quality，1 side polished and size 2″ 0.5 mm wafer (preferred).　～5 pcs each.

price：US＄180/pc for ＜100＞，US＄200/pc for ＜111＞

(100)，(110)，(111) step/ etched Nb-STO substrates，prime quality，1 side polished and size 15mm×15mm×0.5mm (preferred).　～5 pcs each.

price：US＄280/pc for＜100＞，US＄340/pc for ＜110＞，US＄400/pc for＜111＞

shipping charge：US＄50

delivery time：3 weeks

Look forward to your order.

Best regards，

Moyi

0551-5591559 5592566 13955161011

www. kmtcrystal. com

www. kmtfurnace. com

点评：由于是电子信函，在制式的信头中，已经标明是回复哪一封来信，所以信的正文中没有提及。报价时除了给出价格以外，还要说明邮寄费用（shipping charge）和交货期（delivery time）。

Unit 7　Doing Business on the Web

Warming-up Questions:

1. How do your customers find out about you and your products through Internet advertising?

2. How do you sell products through online catalogs and order systems?

3. Can you describe the post-sale services (also mean after-sales services) that you can give your customers electronically?

Related links:

1. http://www. managementhelp. org/infomgnt/e _ cmmrce/e _ cmmrce. htm # anchor1167431

2. http://www. igs. net/~whisper/art16. htm

Companies have been marketing products to customers through traditional media, such as TV, radio, magazines, bulletin boards on street, etc. for decades. Marketing managers take advantage of the characteristics of each medium in implementing their marketing plans. With the increasing popularity and improvement in the technology of the Internet, online business becomes possible. Now marketers have a new medium with its own unique qualities: the Internet. There are four steps when marketing your products.

Presale

Let's say that you are the owner of a small company, and you would like to start using the Internet to grow your business. The first thing you must do is to advertise your products. On the Internet, your main advertising tool is a website with lots of product information. Because customers look for vendors through search tools like Yahoo or Google, make sure your website is located in the search tool catalogs. Another advertising possibility is to send e-mail messages to targeted customers with web link to your web site. You can also place ads at other companies' websites with links to your own site.

Remark

The internet offers many opportunities for conveying your advertising messages to your customers. You can set up an electronic showroom for your customers to browse. Your site can make it easy for customers to order product literature, comparison-shop, or test drive your product's features. You might even offer free sample products. You can also gather information about potential customers. A web bit counter is an electronic device that keeps track of the number of customers that visit your site during a particular time period, and provides limited identity information about them. In fact, some advertising rates are based on the number of people that click on an ad taking them to that advertiser's web page.

Taking the Order

Once your customers have made a selection, you must give them a painless way to order it. Some websites are designed to funnel customers to a salesperson at a retail store or on a toll-free telephone line. This approach may work best for complex products because customers are likely to have questions about such products. Even with simpler products for which online ordering is easy, you might want to provide an option for customers to talk to a salesperson. For people that are uneasy about providing credit card or other personal information online, talking to a live person might spell the difference between making and losing the sale.

To make electronic ordering easy for your customers, your website can display a form on the screen. Customers use the electronic shopping carts which are used at Amazon.com or other online stores to hold their orders until they are ready to check out, just like the shopping cart in a grocery store. A cookie keeps track of customers' selections as they shop. Then these selections appear on their order form when they are ready to check out.

Delivering the Products

After customers place their orders, they will be waiting for the delivery of the products. Delivery for E-commerce purchases has to depend on the size of the product, its nature, urgency and the distance that packet will have to travel. Many products and services cannot be delivered electronically over the Internet, so this step of online commerce usually means tracking the process of goods that are shipped by conventional means, such as transport, post, packet, local delivery.

Of course, a lot of software or information products are sold on line and downloaded with savings in packaging, distribution costs and time for both the supplier and the customer.

Remark

Postsale

Marketing doesn't end with the delivery of the products. Often after customers receive their products, they might want to learn more about the product or ask a question about its functions. To give your customers good service after the sale, you could place common questions and answers on your Web site. You can also provide directions for returning or exchanging the product at your site. To answer more technical questions, you can include a link to the manufacturer's Web site.

Gathering feedback from your customers is always important for helping you improve your products and marketing effort. To gather feedback, you can include a follow-up questionnaire on your Web site to find out about your customers, satisfaction with your company's product and service.

Words and Expressions

market *vt.*	推销
decade *n.*	a period of ten years 十年
characteristic *n.*	特征
implement *vt.*	to carry out or put into practice 实施，贯彻，执行
popularity *n.*	流行，普及
unique *adj.*	being the only one, sole 独一无二的
vendor *n.*	seller 卖主，卖方
opportunity *n.*	a favorable moment or occasion (for doing sth.) 机会，时机
convey *vt.*	to take or carry from one place to another 传送，运送
identity *n.*	who or what a particular person or thing is 身份
painless *adj.*	needing no effort or hard work 不费力的
multimedia *n.*	多媒体
funnel *vt.*	to pass through 漏过
option *n.*	可选择的办法
urgency *n.*	the noun form of urgent 迫切
conventional *adj.*	守旧的，按惯例（习俗）办事的
replacement *n.*	the noun form of replace 替代，代替
manufacturer *n.*	a firm that manufacture goods 制造商，制造公司
feedback *n.*	反馈的意见（信息）
bulletin board	广告牌

Remark

take advantage of	利用
targeted customers	目标消费者
link to	连接，链接
test drive	体验
potential customers	潜在顾客
keep track of	了解……的动态，掌握……的线索
toll-free telephone line	由接电话的人或单位付费的电话
a web bit counter	一种网络计数器
be based on	以……为基础（根据）
a retail store	一家零售商店
check out	结账离开
place an order	下订单
end with	以……结束
follow-up questionnaire	后续（随后）的问卷

Notes

1. **Yahoo and Google**：是普遍使用的搜索引擎。

2. **browser**：浏览器。一种在网上查阅信息时的软件工具。使用它，可以浏览网上各个站点的信息。目前较为流行的浏览器有：Microsoft 的 Internet Explorer，Sun 的 Hot Java 和 Netscape 的 Navigator 等。

3. **A web bit counter is an electronic device that keeps track of the number of customers that visit your site during a particular time period, and provides limited identity information about them.** 网络计数器是一种能记录在一段时间内浏览你的网站的人数，并能提供关于他们的一定的身份信息的一种装置。此句中，第一个 that 引导的是定语从句，修饰 device，第二个 that 引导的还是定语从句，修饰 customers。

4. **Amazon. com**：亚马逊，美国一家著名的网上书店。

5. **cookie**：a small file or part of a file stored on a World Wide Web user's computer, created and subsequently read by a Web site server, and containing personal information (as a user identification code, customized preferences, or a record of pages visited)"点心"文件。互联网浏览器储存在电脑里面的文件夹就被称做 cookies。Cookies 是联网用户计算机硬盘中的一个记录用户个人资料、所用电脑系统的资料和该用户浏览过的网页等资料的资料卡。

Exercises

Reading Comprehension

A. According to the text, answer the following questions.

1. How have been companies marketing products to customers through tradi-

Remark

tional media?

2. How many methods do you know to convey your ads to your customers? What are they?

3. What shall we do to make electronic order easy for customers?

4. Why does online business become possible?

5. According to the author, there are four steps when marketing your products. What are they?

B. Write "T" for true and "F" for false according to the passage.

1. Corporations have been marketing their products through traditional media, such as radio, TV, magazine, and Internet, etc. (　　)

2. If you want to start your business using Internet, the first thing you must do is to advertise your products on line. (　　)

3. On the Internet, the only advertising tool is web sites. (　　)

4. A painless way to take an order is to provide an option for customers to talk to a salesperson. (　　)

5. Delivery for E-commerce purchases has to depend on the size of the product, its nature, urgency and the distance that packet will have to travel. (　　)

Translation

A. Translate the following sentences into Chinese.

1. A web bit counter is an electronic device that keeps track of the number of customers that visit your site during a particular time period, and provides limited identity information about them.

2. Customers use the electronic shopping carts which are used at *Amazon. com* or other online stores to hold their orders until they are ready to check out, just like the shopping cart in a grocery store.

3. To gather feedback, you can include a follow-up questionnaire on your Web site to find out about your customers, satisfaction with your company's products and service.

4. This approach may work best for complex products because customers are likely to have questions about such products.

5. Another advertising possibility is to send e-mail messages to targeted customers with web link to your web site.

B. Translate the following sentences into English.

1. 开发者如何能利用 Windows 2000 新特征？（take advantage of）

2. 合同以失败告终。（end with）

3. 订货之前，我得和老板商量一下。（place an order）

4. 他喜欢了解化学方面一切新发展的情况。（keep track of）

5. 好的项目依赖于扩大贸易。（depend on）

Supplementary Reading

Making People Want to Buy in Your Retail Web Store

What is an on-line retail store? Silly question. It's a place where people can buy things on the Internet, you say. But what is it? A deliberately created environment which causes a customer to want to purchase. The dictionary defines environment as "the complex of physical, chemical, and biotic factors that act upon an organism or an ecological community and ultimately determine its form and survival." Shopping, too, is complex, and relates a great deal to environment, and the intricate experience of desiring, deciding, and taking action. Thinking of shopping as a customer experience rather than a transaction and you begin get the picture.

Experiencing a purchasing environment

When I walk into a local store what do I see? What do I feel? What do I touch? What do I hear? The cushiness of the carpet has something to do with my perception of quality and value. The way aisles are arranged, the lighting, the gentle music, the friendly clerk who asks if I need some help. It all flows together to create an impression, and a desire to either linger and look, or to leave as fast as possible.

On the Internet, Web pages are the store, the entire interface between customer and shop owner. Do the graphics make you feel good about being there or jumpy? Does the balance of color and photos, text and white space look clean and inviting, like a floor that is mopped and buffed every night, and shelves which are dusted and restocked after hours? Can you click on a Real Audio™ icon and hear music or a word from the storeowner? What is the whole effect? How does it make you feel? If you've ever studied the psychology of advertising and purchasing, you know that feelings have a great deal to do with the whole process.

Waiting on Customers

Do you hear a cheery on-line, "May I help you?" I hope not! But you should provide multiple ways for your customers to see what you have to offer. If people can find their way around your store easily, they'll want to purchase there—and return to shop again.

Your customers can't ask a clerk questions about using the product— not in real-time, at least — but they can find lots of applications information posted in your Web store which gives them confidence to buy from you rather than from the corresponding "real" store in their city, where they are used to asking for an explanation before purchasing.

Remark

Words and Expressions

deliberately *adv.*	故意地
biotic *adj.*	生物的
ecological *adj.*	生态学的
ultimately *adv.*	最终
intricate *adj.*	复杂的
cushiness *n.*	轻松赚钱
linger *v.*	逗留
graphics *n.*	图示
jumpy *adj.*	神经质的
mop *v.*	擦，抹
buff *v.*	抛光
cheery *adj.*	愉快的

A Guide to E-mail Writting

还价（counteroffer）

写作要点：还价是由于对对方的条款、价格等方面不满意，寻求新的解决方式而写的信函。用清楚简洁的语言陈述解决方案。

Specimen Letter

Dear Mr. Kong，

Thanks for your quotation submission dated 21 February 2008. Please note that our standard payment term is net 30 days after receipt of goods and invoice and we have used this payment method to deal with your company since 1998. We are a government funded university with sound financial background，you can visit our website at "www.ust.hk" for more information about us. Please consider to offer us credit terms for reducing administration effort. Thank you.

Regards

Estor Kong

Purchasing Office

HKUST

点评：买方陈述自己的优势而使商家不愿意放弃。

credit terms 是赊销付款条件。

Remark

Unit 8　Digital Advertising

Warming-up Questions：

1. How much do you know about the digital advertising?

2. If you are a general manager of a company, how will you advertise your products?

3. Do you like Banner ads ? Why or why not?

Related links：

1. http://advertising. microsoft. com/home/home

2. http://www. 247realmedia. com/EN-US/intel/digital-advertising. html

Listing Your Products on Your Website

The Internet age brings a new way of communication with potential clients. Most companies which are doing e-commerce advertise their products through targeted e-mails and banner ads. When customers search for certain keywords, they will appear. Creating and placing these messages in banner ads and e-mails is a way to draw customers to the company's Web site.

Advertisers collect Demographics (are characteristics of human populations broken down by age, gender, or income etc.) information to help them target their ad messages to particular groups of customers. For example, if your company sells down coats, your advertising would be most effective if you could send it to people who live in the north of China.

In order to target your advertising message to particular customer groups, you can collect demographic information for your customer database through various methods, or even buy the information from other companies. Along with typical demographic information, you can also collect e-mail addresses and interests. For example, if you run a sporting goods store, you can write an e-mail message promoting your camping equipment to all customers between the age of 18 and 30 that like to camp.

The most common type of Internet advertising is to send electronic mail messages to individuals whose names and other information are maintained in a database. E-mail ads are inexpensive, easy to send, and hard to ignore in the recipient's in-

Remark

box. The ads describe the company's products and service, and usually include one or more links to the company's Web site.

E-mail ads can be complete as sent or can contain an embedded hyperlink to a Web site. In fact most e-mail ads are linked to a Web server with much more information. Many of the e-mail messages work best with HTML-enhanced e-mail programs, which are capable of displaying messages with embedded HTML commands that link to web pages.

According to common demographic characteristics, you can electronically group customer e-mail addresses in your database. For example, you could group together all customers who have purchased swimming equipment from your sporting goods store or expressed interest in swimming in a survey. Then when you have a sale on swimming accessories, you can send an e-mail to these customers.

You may use another way to target specific customer groups with an e-mail ad, that is, to advertise with an Internet mailing list service. Internet users subscribe to the service if they are interested in the service's subject, such as sports news, or any of thousands of subjects offered this way. New users generally subscribe by sending an e-mail with the word "subscribe" in it, and then automatically receive all e-mail reports sent to the list of subscribers.

For your sporting goods store, a mailing list service identifies potential customers for you and gives you a way to reach them. People who have subscribed to receive reports about swim would probably be interested in your swimming equipment. If you advertise with this mailing list, your swimming equipment ad will be placed on the e-mail reports that go to the list's subscribers.

Banner Advertising

Banner ads appear on web pages as a rectangular image. Most banner ads contain a link to the advertiser's Web site for the viewer to click. Banner ads can not only snatch the customer's attention but also supply customers with detailed information about the ad's contents in seconds.

Static ads are advertisements that always appear in a given location on the web page, similar to an ad in a magazine or newspaper. These ads appear regardless of the key words used to arrive at the site. Advertisers pay rates based on the number of hits on the Web page containing the ad, with bonus if the viewer clicks on the ad. Check out the URL of a hyperlink in a Web banner ad, and you will usually see extra codes at the end that tell the advertiser where the user came from and/or where to search. The advertiser can use this information to make decisions about future advertising placement.

Remark

Some banner ads are animated, drawing your eyes and increasing the likelihood that you will click on the ad to find more information. These animated GIF ads are often much larger and take longer to load than non-animated ads.

Companies choose to advertise on Web sites that snatch the types of people who would most likely be interested in their products. A computer hardware company's Web site might contain ads by software firms that produce products that run on those computers. In some cases, companies have reciprocal agreements that allow each to put advertisements on the other's Web site. These cooperative ads are pairs of ads placed in complementary sites. Viewers at one site would likely be interested in products at the other site. For example, the PC Connection home page highlights computers made by a certain manufacturer. When you get to that manufacture's Web site, you will find PC Connection listed first among the online sellers.

Search engine sites are natural starting points for users. They contain links to other sites, acting as a doorway or portal. Because popular sites like Yahoo are the top sites for Web activity, they are popular among advertisers that want to catch more viewers.

Entering subject keywords in a search engine brings up an advertisement related to that subject at the top of the search results. These ads are called dynamic ads, because they only appear when users select a particular subject. Advertisers prefer dynamic advertising, because they know the viewer is already interested in topics that pertain to their products.

One way to improve the effectiveness of your advertising message is to use alt-text lines with the ad. Alt-text lines are short phrases that appear in an image's location while the image is downloading.

Banner ads are sold by size, measured in pixel. A pixel is the smallest element on a computer display screen. The most popular ad size is full-banner, which is 468 pixels wide by 60 pixels high, or about six inches wide and one inch high. Other common sizes are 392 pixels by 72 pixels, etc.

Advertising rates are usually based on CPM, or cost per thousand impressions. On the Web, the number of impressions is the number of hits, or times the page has been accessed.

The more targeted the audience, the more expensive the ad rates. To minimize the cost of advertising, two or three companies might share a rotation ad on a given Web page. A rotation ad is a banner ad that rotates between advertisers. Each time the page is loaded or refreshed, the advertiser changes. Usually the sponsors of the rotation ads are named at the bottom of the Web page.

One popular portal site charges $24~38 CPM for general rotation ads that ap-

Remark

pear at the top of pages on the site. Advertisers can reserve keywords for a certain period of time at a rate of $70~85 CPM. A reserved keyword means that whenever the viewer searches for that keyword, one advertiser's ad appears. Advertisers receive daily reports about hits on their sites.

Each Web site has its own advertising rates. As a potential advertiser, you can negotiate with the provider for favorable rates. You can lower the CPM cost by agreeing to a longer advertising contract.

Pop-up ads are ads that appear in a different browser window on top of the base Web page that remains open in the background. Pop-under ads appear underneath the current Web page and are viewed when you close the main browser window. A pop-up or pop-under ad can grab a viewer's attention more than a normal banner ad within a Web page, and therefore earns a premium advertising rate. To remove the ad from view, users must close the extra window by clicking the Close button, probably causing the ad to remain in users' minds longer than other types of ads.

Promoting Your Site

You need to deliver your message to potential clients. Most companies doing e-commerce try to lure buyers to a Web site. How do you get that URL out to world?

• Make your business name part of your URL. For example, see www. mengniu. com. cn.

• Include your URL in e-mail messages sent to prospective clients.

• Put a banner ad on another popular Web site that potential clients are likely to visit.

• Present your URL to the major portals, such as Yahoo, Sohu, Sina, and Ebay. When clients search using keywords relevant to your business, your site will come up in the list of Web sites that match their search criteria.

• Advertise your Web address in other media, such as television.

• Have your Web address on your business cards, stationery, and other documents.

• Advertise your Web address on billboards, trucks, and other places visible to potential clients.

• Use a paid service to promote your site.

• Hire an advertising agency to promote your site.

• Just wait till the search engines' Web spiders find your site and adds it to a search engine's catalog or index.

It is particularly important to make sure that your Web site contains appropriate keywords that Web spiders can pick up. Select good descriptive words that will

Remark

be programmed into the home page file by a Web developer. Make sure the title of your site is a good description of the site. The site title appears in the title bar of the browser when customers visit your site and is frequently listed in the search engine results. The location of your title bar depends on your browser: Some title bars are at the top of the screen and others are at the bottom. A Web developer can place the title text into your site's home page file.

Words and expressions

effective *adj.*		有效的，有影响的
database *n.*	an organized body of related information	数据库
various *adj.*	of many different kinds of purposefully arranged but lacking any uniformity	各种各样的
individual *adj.* & *n.*		个别的；个人；个体
ignore *v.*	to give little or no attention to	不顾，不理，忽视
recipient *n.*	a person who gets something	接收人，收信人
embed *v.*	fix or set securely or deeply	使插入，使嵌入，［计］嵌入
hyperlink *n.*		［计］超链接
command *n.*		［计］Dos 命令；引用辅助命令处理器
accessory *n.* & *adj.*		附件；附属的，辅助的
subscribe *v.*		捐献；订阅
automatically *adv.*	in a mechanical manner; by a mechanism	自动地
rectangular *n.*	having four right angles	矩形
snatch *v.*	to grasp hastily or eagerly	夺取；侥幸获得
static *adj.*	not active or moving	静态的
rate *n.*		等级；价格
bonus *n.*	anything that tends to arouse	红利，奖金
animated *adj.*		有生气的，活泼的
reciprocal *adj.*		相互的
highlight *v.*		加强，强调；［计］醒目
rotate *v.*		（使）旋转
negotiate *v.*		商议，谈判，交涉
browser *n.*		浏览器
premium *n.*	additional payment	奖金，额外，补贴
lure *n.* & *v.*	anything that serves as an enticement	饵，诱惑
	provoke someone to do something through promises or persuasion	引诱，诱惑
communicate with		与……交流

search for	寻找，搜寻
regardless of	不顾，不惜，不注意
relate to	有关，涉及
come up	上来，上升，抬头
add to	增加到……上，添加
pick up	见到，听出，收听到
act as	充当，担任
bring up	提出……以供注意或考虑；谈到

Notes

1. **HTML**: a set of tags and rules (conforming top SGML) for using them in developing hypertext documents

2. **URL(Uniform Resource Locator)**: the address of a web page on the world wide web

3. **ALT-text**: short text phrases that appear in an image's location while the image is downloading

4. **pixel**: the smallest discrete component of an image or picture on a CRT screen (usually a colored dot)

Exercises

Reading Comprehension

According to the text, answer the following questions.

1. How do you collect demographic information for your customer database?
2. What is a static ad?
3. Why are search engine sites often called portal sites?
4. To minimize the cost of advertising, what do some companies do?
5. How do you let people know your URL?

Translation

A. Translate the following sentences into Chinese.

1. In order to target your advertising message to particular customer groups, you can collect demographic information for your customer database through various methods, or even buy the information from other companies.

2. The most common type of Internet advertising is to send electronic mail messages to individuals whose names and other information are maintained in a database.

3. Static ads are advertisements that always appear in a given location on the

web page, similar to an ad in a magazine or newspaper.

4. Some banner ads are animated, drawing your eyes and increasing the likelihood that you will click on the ad to find more information.

5. A pop-up or pop-under ad can grab a viewer's attention more than a normal banner ad within a Web page, and therefore earns a premium advertising rate.

B. Translate the following sentences into English with the given words.

1. 在信息时代，人们经常通过网络互相交流。(communicate with)

2. 电子商务是以网络信息系统为基础的。(base on)

3. 广告能起到促销的作用。(act as)

4. 随着网络技术的日益完善，各种与网络有关商业活动出现了。(along with)

5. 如果你登录相关的网站，你就会看到你需要的图片。(pick up)

Supplementary Reading

Advertising

Advertising is a way of bringing information to the public for the purpose of selling a product, a service, an idea, or an event. All advertising is aimed to encourage people to take certain action, such as buying a product, ordering a service, joining an organization, or attending a meeting.

In a modern society, everyone uses advertising in one way or another. e. g., a person may get a job by answering an ad in a newspaper.

Product advertising is closely related to selling and, in most cases, is part of an overall selling program. Such ads are aimed to make people familiar with products and eager to buy them.

Advertising has certainly played an important part in making modern goods and services available to the public. It encourages consumers to accept such new products as cars, telephones, computers and fridges. Each ad is paid by a person, a group, an organization, or a company seeking to achieve its goals. With the economy expanding, large corporations are spending huge amounts of money to improve their brands and influence buyers through many types of Advertising Media. .

The more important types of advertising media are newspaper, televisions, radios, direct mails, magazines, the Internet, billboards and word of mouth. Other types of media include fliers, posters, balloons, tickets, movies, vehicles, etc.

Newspaper ads are low in cost and can be prepared within limited time. Retailers use such ads to promote the product or service for the local market. The disadvantages are: its life is short and colour is poor.

TV commercial is generally considered the most effective mass-market advertising format. It is mainly used by big firms with well-selling products.

Remark

Advertising over radio is inexpensive in terms of preparation and targets certain types of audiences (e. g. taxi drivers) in local marketing.

Direct mail advertising sends letters, fliers and catalogues to people's home. It is very effective if the advertiser can get a qualified database of the targeted people. The shortcoming of doing so is that sometimes people treat it as a junk mail and throw it away without reading.

Magazine advertising is mainly used to attract specific audiences. It can make the most of color, and have a longer life than that of TV or newspaper ads.

Advertising on Internet is usually placed on web pages that have interesting contents. Prices of Web-based advertising space are dependent on the "relevance" of the surrounding Web contents.

Billboards show large advertisements aimed at passing pedestrians and drivers. Such ads usually use distinctive color pictures and are simple to read but limited in the message they can convey.

Word of mouth can provide good exposure at minimal cost. So many sellers ask their satisfied customers to recommend their product or services to their friends. It is regarded as one of the most effective tools for promotion.

Advertising used to promote commercial goods and services can also be used to inform, educate and motivate the public about serious non-profitable issued, such as AIDS and environment protection. Advertising when used in the public interest is a powerful educational tool which is capable of reaching and motivating large audiences.

If you want to advertise, you may organize advertising yourself or use an advertising agency. Some small companies choose to handle the advertising themselves as they are familiar with their product or services, targeted customers, and the market.

As the company grows and starts to promote many different kinds of goods or services, they hand over the job of advertising to professional ad agencies, which can provide them one-stop service including writing the script, creating artwork and selecting the media. And they normally do a better job in advertising.

Words and Expressions

overall *adj.*	总体的，全部的，综合的
billboard *n.*	宣传栏，广告板
pedestrian *n.*	行人
script *n.*	剧本，脚本，讲稿
hand over	移交，让与
mass-market	大众市场

Remark

A Guide to E-mail Writting

付款方式 （payment）

写作要点：在与对方讨论付款方式的时候，一定要清楚地阐明自己的要求，并对自己的公司或企业做些介绍，以证明自己的实力。

Specimen Letter

Dear Prof. xu，

Thank you for your e-mail about payment issue.

We have no arrangement with our forwarder to make payment on our behalf. We are world wide known University and our researchers received Nobel Prize. You can visit our web site at http：//www. technion. ac. il/. Our supplier generally granted us payment terms of net 30 days. In order to simplify the process we suggest you the "Cash against Documents" terms：the AWB will be consigned to our bank. In order to obtain endorsement from our bank we will have to give instructions for payment. This kind of arrangement ensures you that you will receive payment and we will receive the goods ordered.

Kindly recheck if this is acceptable to you.

Best Regards，

Solange Elishav

Purchase Dept.

Technion-Israel Institute of Technology

Technion City

32000-Haifa

Israel

Tel：972-4-8294156

Fax：972-4-8221680

E-mail：elishav@dp. technion. ac. il

　　点评：这封邮件的目的试图在争取 KMT 公司给予 30 天放账期限，邮件的书写者在信中表述了他们是一所世界知名的大学，特别指出他们的研究人员是诺贝尔奖的获得者，以求获得供应商的认可。

　　"Cash against Documents" 是一种付款方式，交单付现 （CAD） 即凭单据付款。

　　Technion：以色列技术学院是以色列的最高学府。

Unit 9　E-mail Application in E-commerce

Warming-up Questions:

1. What should you pay attention to when you send an e-mail to your business partners?

2. What are the differences between e-mails and conventional letters?

3. Discuss with your partner what a spam (junk mail) is ?

Related links:

1. http: // harvardbusinessonline. hbsp. harvard. edu/hbsp/index. jsp; jses-sionid=AN0KTVBU2UXMGAKRGWDSELQBKE0YIISW? _ requestid=54075

2. http: //www. managementhelp. org/commskls/netiquet/netiquet. htm

E-mail, the shortened form for electronic mail, is one of the most popularly used functions in the Internet. It is the modern communication service, by which you can send a message to any person in the world who has an e-mail address within a short time. E-mail message can be the same as a letter or can include sound and pictures as well. It has more contents and carries more information than a letter.

An e-mail has the following advantages. (1) It can be communicated as fast as international phone call and fax. (2) It is cheaper than an international phone call and fax. (3) The message can be sent easily. (4) It is a 24-hour service and the message can be received unattended.

How to Writting an E-mail

An e-mail message is a lot like a regular letter or memo. It contains a heading with the receiver's address, the sender's address, the subject of the message, and the date and time when the message is sent. Following the heading is the greeting and then the body or text of the message itself. You can also choose to add a signature block to the end of the message.

When you receive an e-mail message, you will see the additional text in the heading area, reflecting the handling of your message by the outgoing and incoming mail systems. As new messages arrive from your ISP or network server, they are stored in your Inmailbox, or Inbox.

Remark

Inquiry and Quotation

The negotiation of a commodity transaction often begins with an inquiry. The buyer usually makes an inquiry to the supplier querying about the articles he wants to order. What the buyer inquires about includes not only the prices but other terms of transaction. The buyer may ask the supplier to send him catalogs or sample books. And sometimes the buyer may also list the quality, quantity, specifications and the time of delivery, in order that the supplier can offer accordingly.

An inquiry can be sent by web inquiry form, or e-mail, or fax, or telegram, or telex, or telephone. The reply to an inquiry should be prompt and courteous and cover all the information asked for.

Putting a Purchase Order

A purchase order is a proposal of terms and conditions of buying or selling a certain commodity. In general, it is the seller who offers the sale of certain commodities to the buyer. Such wording as offer, offer firm, quote is mostly used.

There are two kinds of offers firm offer and non-firm offer. A firm offer is made when a seller promises to sell goods at a stated price within a stated period of time. A firm offer should be definite, complete, clear and of final in its wording. It should include the following: the name of the commodity, quality, quantity and specifications, details of prices, terms of payment, date of delivery and the period for which the offer is valid. But a non-firm offer might contain fewer terms. Such kind of offer is not binding on the seller.

Making Complaints

Mistakes may occur in day-to-day business, and these give cause for complaints. There might have been a misunderstanding about the goods to be supplied; perhaps damage may have occurred during delivery, and so on. A disappointed customer cannot be put off with mere apologies: he is entitled to know how the mistakes will be remedied, when he will receive the goods ordered, when he will receive a replacement for his defective machine, or if it can be repaired quickly.

If you are not satisfied with either the goods or service or other things, you can send a complaint letter to the seller. Ordinarily, the purpose of writing a letter of complaint is to get better service. The more specific your letter is, the easier it will be for your correspondent to handle your complaint.

Remark

Words and Expressions

application *n.*　　the act of putting something to use 应用；申请

unattended *adj.*	无人照料的，没人照看的
memo *n.*	备忘录
signature *n.*	the act of signing one's name 签字，签名
inquiry *n.*	inquiring 询问，打听
quotation *n.*	报价，行情
negotiation *n.*	an act of negotiating 谈判，协商
additional *adj.*	附加的，额外的
transaction *n.*	a piece of business（一笔）交易，业务
terms *n.*（pl.）	条件，条款
specifications *n.*（pl.）	规格，规范明细表
accordingly *adv.*	相应地
courteous *adj.*	有礼貌的
definite *adj.*	明确的，确实的，一定的
wording *n.*	用词，措辞
complaint *n.*	抱怨，投诉
mere *adj.*	only 仅仅
defective *adj.*	有缺陷的，有毛病的
specific *adj.*	明确的，确切的
correspondent	通信者；符合的，一致的
long points	优点，长处
and... as well	也一样
make an inquiry	询问
query about	询价，询问
in general	一般的说，总的来说
day-to-day business	日常的业务
put off	推迟
be entitled to do	有权利做某事，有享受的……资格
be satisfied with	对满意

Notes

1. **ISP**：是 Internet Service Provider 的缩写，网络服务提供商
2. **network server**：网络服务器
3. **Inmailbox, or Inbox**：a computer folder devoted to incoming e-mail 收件箱
4. **firm offer and non-firm offer**：实盘和虚盘

Exercises

Reading Comprehension

A. According to the text，answer the following questions.

1. What are the advantages of an e-mail?
2. What does a supplier usually inquire about?

Remark

3. What is a firm order and non-firm order?

4. Under what kind of circumstances will you send a complaint letter to sellers?

5. What items should be included in writing an inquiry letter?

B. Write "T" for true and "F" for false according to the text.

1. E-mail message can be same a letter, but it can not include sound and pictures. It has more contents and carries more information than a letter. (　　)

2. Ordinarily, the purpose of writing a letter of complaint is to get more money and better service. (　　)

3. A purchase order is a proposal of terms and conditions of buying or selling a certain commodity. In general, it is the seller who offers the sale of certain commodities to the buyer. (　　)

4. The negotiation of a commodity transaction often begins with an inquiry. (　　)

5. The reply to an inquiry may be prompt and polite and cover all the information asked for. (　　)

Translation

A. Translate the following sentences into Chinese.

1. What the buyer inquires about includes not only the prices but other terms of transaction.

2. And sometimes the buyer may also list the quality, quantity, specifications and the time of delivery, in order that the supplier can offer accordingly.

3. A purchase order is a proposal of terms and conditions of buying or selling a certain commodity.

4. There might have been a misunderstanding about the goods to be supplied; perhaps damage may have occurred during delivery, and so on.

5. It should include the following: the name of the commodity, quality, quantity and specifications, details of prices, terms of payment, date of delivery and the period for which the offer is valid.

B. Translate the following sentences into English.

1. 我们越多地使用这个软件，就越发地发现它很方便。（the more... the more）

2. 顾客有权力知道产品的生产日期。（be entitled to do）

3. 顾客对他们公司的售后服务非常满意。（be satisfied with）

4. 认识从实践开始。（begin with）

5. 任何一个买家都不希望自己购买的产品被推迟发货。（put off）

Supplementary Reading

The Basics of a Successful E-Mail Marketing Effort

The most common question I get as an e-mail marketing consultant is along the

Remark

lines of, "Can you get me a list of e-mail addresses of real estate agencies in the Cleveland area?" In almost every case, this is the wrong question to ask. Success in e-mail marketing does not come from renting the right list and blasting[3] out an ad to everyone on it. The basis of successful e-mail marketing is the development of your own house e-mail list or lists. A "rented" e-mail list only benefits you one time. Your own e-mail list allows you to develop a long-term relationship with your on-line audience—to communicate with and market to them over and over.

In building your own e-mail list, you'll need to cover these bases:

1. Decide what audience you're trying to reach and what you have to offer them.

2. What kind of relationship do you want with the recipients of your e-mailings?

3. Determine what format your e-mailings will take—ads, newsletter, deals and specials, company announcements and press releases, discussion list?

4. Will you offer HTML e-mail, or just text?

5. Who will handle the creative aspects of your mailings—writing, copywriting, editing? Will you need to outsource this or other functions?

6. Set goals and make a specific plan: How often do you plan to mail? How long will your messages be? How many addresses do you want on your list in six months? One year? Two years?

7. How will you collect e-mail addresses—from Web forms, registration or subscription forms, trade shows, during telephone contacts or sales calls?

8. Use outside lists to build your in-house list. To recruit list members, rent an opt-in[7] list to send out an announcement, or take out an ad in an e-mail newsletter or discussion list.

9. Make sure that all your lists are opt-in—that all recipients have explicitly given you permission to mail to them. Make it easy for list members to unsubscribe.

10. What will be your technical requirements, given the volume of E-mail you'll be sending over the long run? Consider bandwidth, e-mail server software, list management software, hardware requirements, management of bad addresses and similar factors.

11. Will you host your lists in-house, or go with a list hosting company?

In E-mail marketing, trust is the key element. Never abuse your relationship with your list members. Make sure that the e-mail you send them is relevant and offers value.

Words and expressions

consultant *n.*	顾问
real estate	房地产
blast *v.*	呈现
recipient *n.*	接受者

Remark

outsource v.	外包
subscription n.	订阅
opt-in	决定参加
unsubscribe v.	注销
bandwidth n.	带宽

A Guide to E-mail Writting

网上广告（online advertisement）

Your Business Gateway To World Buyers & Suppliers

B2B Global Trading Marketplace for Electric/Electronic Components，Parts，Appliances & Equipments.

Welcome your attend to our B2B Website Global Marketplace Memberships Service for dealers，resellers，brokers，distributors and manufacturers that is connecting professional Global Buyers/Sellers who are looking to Buy，Sell and Trade mainstream or hard-to-find Electric/Electronic Components，Parts，Appliances and Equipments.

Dear Prof. xu，

Our B2B Website Global Trading Marketplace Online！It is a good opportunity for entering into global Electric/Electronics markets which you can upload your in-stock Electric/Electronic products for sale.

• Login New Members/Post your Stock/Daily Requirements/Daily Hot Offers

• Login at our B2B Global Marketplace and POST YOUR STOCK/REQUIREMENTS/HOT OFFERS.

Send your Stock List to our powerful database of B2B Global Marketplace for global buyers.

We look forward to have your attention through our B2B Global Trading Marketplace geared to improve your business in the near future. Very attractive membership price：One day cost only～USD1.

If you are interesting to attend our memberships，please describe your company name，address，Tel，Fax No. contact person name To Email us：charliez@ms77. hinet. net（BUT DO NOT reply to other email address that we just can not receive it！）

Best regards，

B2B Global Trading Marketplace

Service Manager/Charliez

点评：E-mail 广告的促销作用是不可忽视的，花很少的钱去赢得市场，并要求语言简洁有吸引力。广告的第一句话尤为重要。如：Your Business Gateway To World Buyers & Suppliers，让读信人眼前一亮，在怀疑世界上还有这等好事的同时有进一步想去了解它的倾向。这无疑已经达到了广告的目的。E-mail 广告的难度是如何避免你的广告对象把你的邮件作为垃圾处理掉。最后切记，诚信和优良的服务是支撑广告成功的最终力量。

Remark

Unit 10　Global E-commerce

Warming-up Questions:

1. How does the internet bring customers and sellers together, even though they are not in the same place?

2. How can a company take advantage of its own "private internet" to manage business around the world?

3. How do companies use the Internet to do business virtually anywhere in the world?

Related links:

1. http: // harvardbusinessonline. hbsp. harvard. edu/hbsp/resource _ centers/ global _ business. jsp? N=512348

2. http: // www. igs. net/~whisper/art16. htm

Electronic commerce is a revolution that is sweeping across the world, changing the way we do business, the way we shop and even the way we think. More and more businesses are planning to engage in electronic commerce. E-commerce becomes global.

Doing Business Anywhere, Anytime

Today, business is a global activity. Multinational corporations have branches, plants, and business partners all over the world. They may gather raw materials in one country, refine them in another, assemble them into finished goods in yet another country, and sell their finished products virtually everywhere. And although English is the dominant language in North America, The United Kingdom, and a few other countries, most multinational firms must be able to conduct business in many languages. Large firms offer versions of their web sites in several languages, available by clicking a link. Some search engine sites have international versions that highlight sites in that particular country, often in the country's language.

Lowering Geographic Barrier

In the past, a company was operated by creating products, running facilities that

Remark

manufacture the products, a distribution system that delivers the products, stores that display the goods, and a sales force that promotes the products. In most cases, the company's customers were primarily from the same geographic region.

But the Internet is reducing the need for some of these traditional business activities. If your company has an e-commerce site on the Web, customers can reach you for free from just about anywhere. You don't need a retail store or salespeople to call on customers. You don't even have to accept sales orders in person any longer. The Internet lowers geographic barriers by supporting low-cost communication between suppliers, employees, business partners, and customers.

Asynchronous Worldwide Activities

Traditionally, a business transaction could occur only if the business and customers were in the same place at the same time. You and the business were synchronized in time and place. To do business, the company facilities would have to be near to customers and open when the customers wanted to buy goods. If the company wanted to sell to a larger area, it would need multiple facilities.

On the Internet, business activities can be asynchronous—not synchronized in time and place. Internet companies can accept orders whenever customers want to place them, and online catalogs are always up-to-date. Customers and sellers can transact business at different times and in different locations. An airline customer can check flight schedules and make reservations online at any time, not just when the airline reservation center is able to answer the phone call from that customer.

Online International Business Information

When you are planning to do business with someone from another country, there is a lot of research to do. The Internet is a network of public networks, generally available everywhere around the world. When information is placed on the Internet, it is usually considered public information and freely accessible. If you were an international businessman, you could access critical information about other countries through Internet. You could learn about the culture and business practices of a particular region, along with demographic statistics, transportation capabilities, industrial resources, and so forth. You could begin to develop business relationships before you ever set foot in the country.

Words and Expressions

revolution *n.*　　　　革命，变革
sweep *vi.*　　　　横扫，掠过

Remark

multinational *adj.*	多国的
refine *vt.*	净化，精炼
assemble *vt.*	装配，组合
virtually *adv.*	almost，very nearly 实际上，事实上
dominant *adj.*	最重要的
version *n.*	样式，种类，版本
available *adj.*	可得到的，可利用的
access *vt.*	进入，得到
demographic *adj.*	人口统计学的
statistics *n.*	统计数字，统计资料
facilities *n.*	设施，设备
distribution *n.*	分发，配送
geographic *adj.*	of geography 地域的，地理的
lower *vt.*	降低
synchronize *vt.*	使同时发生
asynchronous *adj.*	不同时的，异步的
up-to-date *adj.*	fashionable，latest 流行的，时尚的
schedule *n.* （*esp.*）	时刻表
accessible *adj.*	容易达到的，易接近的
across the world	全世界
raw materials	原材料
search engine	搜索引擎
engage in	从事于，忙于
in most cases	在大多数情况下
make reservations	预订
at any time	在任何时候
multinational corporations	多国公司
industrial resources	工业资源
and so forth	等等

Notes

1. **Electronic commerce** is a revolution that is sweeping across the world, changing the way we do business, the way we shop and even the way we think. 电子商务是一次席卷整个世界的革命，它改变了我们做生意的方式，我们购物的方式以及我们思维的方式。在这个句子中，that 引导定语从句，changing... 是现在分词短语做状语，三个并列的 the way 后面都是省略了关系代词 that 或 in which 的定语从句。

2. **The United Kingdom**：The United Kingdom of Great Britain and Northern

Ireland（大不列颠及北爱尔兰）联合王国，在不太正式的场合，可以用 the UK，代表英国。

3. **public networks**：大众网络。

Exercises

Reading Comprehension

A. According to the text answer the following questions.

1. Why does e-commerce become global nowadays?

2. How does e-commerce change our way of thinking?

3. Would you like to give an example to show how to do transactions through Internet?

4. What is the function of a search engine?

5. What should you do when you want to do business with people in a foreign country?

B. Write "T" for true and "F" for false according to the text.

1. In the past, the company's customers were primarily from the same geographic region. （　　）

2. The internet is not reducing the need for some of these traditional business activities. （　　）

3. The internet lowers geographic barriers by supporting low-cost communication between suppliers, employees, business partners, and customers. （　　）

4. When you are planning to do business with someone from another country, there is a little research to do. （　　）

5. Traditionally, a business transaction could occur if the business and customer were in the same place at the same time. （　　）

Translation

A. Translate the following sentences into Chinese.

1. Electronic commerce is a revolution that is sweeping across the world, changing the way we do business, the way we shop and even the way we think.

2. They may gather raw materials in one country, refine them in another, assemble them into finished goods in yet another country, and sell their finished products virtually everywhere.

3. Some search engine sites have international versions that highlight sites in that particular country, often in the country's language.

4. Internet companies can accept orders whenever customers want to place them, and online catalogs are always up-to-date.

Remark

5. You could learn about the culture and business practices of a particular region, along with demographic statistics, transportation capabilities, industrial resources, and so forth.

B. Translate the following sentences into English.

1. 越来越多的人从事与网络相关的工作。(engage in)

2. 许多原材料输出到外国。(raw material)

3. 多数情况下，人们能够通过网络购买到自己喜欢的商品。(in most cases)

4. 他是一家零售店的销售经理。(a retail store)

5. 如果你想买到打折的机票，最好的方法是你提前预订。(make reservations)

Supplementary Reading

About eMarketer

eMarketer is "The First Place to Look" for market research and trend analysis on Internet, e-business, online marketing, media and emerging technologies. eMarketer aggregates and analyzes information from over 3, 000 sources, and brings it together in analyst reports, daily research articles and the most comprehensive database of e-business and online marketing statistics in the world.

With eMarketer, you understand the growth and impact of the Internet. Plus, you stay ahead of the curve on new trends such as blogs, social networking, podcasting, mobile marketing, and many others that are profoundly affecting the business landscape.

eMarketer's Core Expertise

eMarketer's core expertise lies in researching and sorting vast amounts of publicly available information, and objectively compiling and analyzing this information into widely read reports, articles and newsletters. Our information products help business executives worldwide make smarter, faster decisions about online marketing, emerging technologies and e-business.

Dedicated Team

Our team of researchers and analysts comb through web sites, data repositories and government statistics, uniquely providing a 360-degree overview of available data, combined with original analysis that is quickly accessible, comprehensive, objective, actionable, cost-effective and, most of all, intelligent.

A Trusted Resource

eMarketer serves as a trusted, third-party resource, cutting through the clutter and hype—helping businesses make sense of the e-business numbers and trends. eMarketer's products and services help companies make better, more informed business decisions by:

Streamlining e-business research sources and reducing costs

Remark

Eliminating critical data gaps

Providing an objective, bird's eye view of the entire e-business landscape

Better deploying and sharing information across the company

Building solid business cases backed up by hard data

Reducing business risk

Saving valuable time

Notes

Podcaste：由 iPod（苹果 MP3 播放器）和 broadcasting（广播）组合而成。它是一种新的技术，是 Rss 技术与 MP3 播放器结合的产物，简单地说，就是把预先录制的 MP3 音频文件发布在 Blog 上，利用相关的 RSS 订阅软件（如 iPodder），你可以定制并将这些 MP3 文件自动下载到本地电脑上播放。

Words and expressions

aggregatev *v.*	聚集、集合
comprehensive *adj.*	全面地、广泛的
expertise *n.*	专门的技术
comb through	梳理
repositories *n.*	储藏库
clutter *n*	混乱
hype *n.*	骗局
bird's eye view	鸟瞰
deploy *v.*	展开、配置
backed up	支持
hard data	翔实的数据

A Guide to E-mail Writting

国际电汇付款信息填报（payment form)

写作要点：下面的表格来自 KMT 的一笔实际操作项目，在国际电子商务活动中大多采用 Wire Transfer Payment，因此填写下面的表格是必须要做的工作，要求学生根据该表格给出的内容自行完成此项工作。通过下面的填表练习，了解国际电子商务贸易支付方法和必须引起注意的环节。

University of Alberta　　　　　　　　**Wire Transfer Payment**

Request

Complete and submit with the applicable Special Payment Request Form (s) to:

Financial Services Cheque Production-3rd floor administration bldg. , Edmonton-AB T6G 2M7

Remark

> **IMPORTANT**: Confirm if the vendor/payee's financial institution requires the use of an intermediary bank to complete a wire funds transfer from the Royal band of Canada (the University's banking institution). Note service charges may apply. These may be charged back to your unit and/or the transfer amount could be reduced with the payee/vendor receiving less than the request payment amount.

Vendor/Payee Information

Vendor Name: _____

Street Address: _____

City, Province/State: _____

Country, Postal/Zip code: _____

Phone Number: _____

Currency: CAD ☐ USD ☐ Other ☐ _____

(if 'Other' Specify)

Vendor/Payee's Bank Information

Primary Bank   Intermediary Bank

(if applicable—see note above)

Beneficiary Name: _____   _____

Bank Name: _____   _____

Bank Address: _____   _____

City, Province/State: _____   _____

Country, Postal/Zip Code: _____   _____

Bank to Bank Details:

Account Number: _____   _____

Bank Number: _____   _____

Transit/Branch Number: _____   _____

SWIFT #: _____   _____

IBAN #: _____   _____

(Or if other bank ID, choose one) ABA ☐ Chips ☐ Other ☐ ABA ☐ Chips ☐ Other ☐

Vendor Payment Details: _____

_____

Should you have any questions please contact Financial Services' wire Payments Coordinator at （780）492-3000 Ext. 2251.

注：SWIFT ♯：SWIFT 又称环球同业银行金融电讯协会，是国际银行同业间的国际合作组织。当前信用证的格式主要都是采用 SWIFT 电文。

IBAN ♯：（The International Bank Account Number）国际银行账号，中国的大多银行是没有 IBAN 号的。

点评：通常国际间电汇付款结算业务需要 vendor 提供详细的付款信息，即完成上述表格的填写。要求收款人（卖家）必须向付款人提供你的银行 SWIFT 号码、银行账号、银行地址、收款人等信息等，以保证资金的安全流转。要注意重要提示中的小字体，那些地方常常会给你带来意想不到的麻烦。

Remark

Unit 11 Creating your Web Site

Warming-up Questions:
1. What are the basic components of a web site?
2. What is the difference between Internet and Intranet?

Related links:
1. http: //www. clipartconnection. com
2. http: //www. make-a-web-site. com/

Your Electronic Commerce Web Site

This lesson discusses the components of an e-commerce Web site. You will learn how a business Web site works and the methods that are available to you for developing the site. You will even develop an online store in this lesson. Then you will learn how to register your domain name and submit your site's URL to the major Web browsers.

Making Your Web Debut

Creating a Web site is actually much simpler than most people think. Of course, building an effective Web site requires a touch of artistic creativity and some energetic work to keep it fresh. Simple Web sites are straightforward to build and publish on a Web server.

Here are the components of e-commerce Web sites that you will learn about in this lesson.

- Text files with embedded HTML commands
- Images, usually, GIF or JPG files
- Web server hardware and software to hold the text files and images
- A connection to the internet or an intranet
- Optional programs called scripts that contain instructions for the Web server
- A database server supporting the online catalog (optional)
- An internal search engine to locate information in the Web site (optional)

Many organizations hire a consultant or advertising company to design and

Remark

build the site. These individuals are called Web developers. If you have the technical knowledge and some artistic talent, you can do it yourself. The online stores at Yahoo make it easy to build your own Web site, which Yahoo will host for a low monthly fee. Or, you can purchase Web package software that helps you create an e-commerce site by simply answering a series of questions.

You need to promote your site so that potential customers can find it on the Internet. We will look into ways to submit your site's URL to the major search engines, and other ways to let people know your site exists.

Components of a Web Site

Basically, a Web site consists of a few text files containing special HTML formatting commands and a Web server computer to host your site. The Web server runs special software that sends out the HTML files to users whose browsers request them. Your Web server will need a connection to the Internet or an intranet. An e-commerce site will also need software to process payments, such as credit cards. Let's take a closer look at each part of a Web site.

- **HTML Files**

The language used to create most Web pages is HTML (hypertext markup language). This simple language adds formatting tags to the basic text of the page. HTML tags are computer codes that tell your Web browser how to display information on your screen. HTML tags are used to indicate such features as bold, character size, font color, hyperlinks, and images. Each tag is sandwiched between angle brackets.

Although it is possible to program Web pages manually using HTML tags, development software tools called Web editors can insert the tags for you, simplifying the task of coding home pages. There are many HTML primers available on the Internet. You will take a look at one in the first step-by-step.

- **Image Files**

As you have already seen throughout the Web sites featured in this book, most use graphic images to enhance the design of Web pages. These images come from a variety of sources, including clip art, photographs, and other software applications. Clip art is a collection of electronic drawings, pictures, and icons, created for use in Web pages and other documents. You can also purchase professional images from online sources, often simplifying the process of finding appropriate graphics for your site. Many Web sites contain free clip art that you can use at your own site. Check out clipartconnection. com for thousands of clip art files.

Remark

• **Web Editor**

You can build your own Web site using Web editor software to create the HT-ML file. A Web editor looks like a word-processing program. In it, you can type the contents of your Web page and then select various formatting options. The Web editor program inserts the necessary HTML tags.

The advantage of a Web editor is the ease with which you can build the features of your Web page. Advanced features such as tables and forms are easy to create and place with Web editor software such as Microsoft FrontPage or Netscape Composer.

When you finish designing, you can save the HTML file with. htm or HTML as the file extension. Then you can transfer the file to the Web server using file transfer protocol (FTP), a standard method for copying files from one computer to another over the Internet.

• **Web Server**

A Web Server is a computer that stores the HTML and graphic files that make a Web site. When your browser requests a Web page stored at the server, the Web server sends the appropriate HTML and graphic files over the Internet to your machine for display on the screen. When the organization hosts a Web site, it stores the associated Web pages on its server. Specialized software on the Web server can track users and gather statistics about visits to your Web site.

• **Internet Connection**

Unlike your personal computer's occasional modern connection to the Internet, the Web server computer needs to have a full-time Internet connection. That is, the server must be available 24/7 (24 hours a day, 7 days a week), whenever someone might request a Web page. Few companies host their own Web site unless they have a full-time connection, which can cost anywhere from $ 60 per month to $ 1, 000 or more, depending on the size of the Web site, the connection speed, and the amount of data transferred.

Web sites as part of the monthly fee. You can also find other sources to host your Web site. Most colleges provide free Web hosting space to their students for personal Web sites.

• **Internal Search Tool**

Most large Web sites include an internal search tool that can be used to look for information on that site. They work just like the search engines that you can access at Yahoo and Google, with keyword searching capability. These search tools

Remark

catalog new material as it is added to the Web site, constantly updating an index of relevant keywords in the search database. For instance, the University of Texas-EI Paso uses a private version for internal searches.

- **Database Server**

Companies often store product catalogs and other useful information in electronic databases on a company server. When the company wants to add a product to the catalog or change a product's stock quantity, it simply makes the changes in the database. If the company Web site links to the database on the company server, then a Web customer can look up a product in the online catalog, and any changes will be reflected there. The company doesn't have to make the changes on the Web site, too. When a customer requests something in the catalog, the Web site simply calls up the company catalog database, retrieves the desired information, and formats it for display on the customer's screen.

- **Web Hosting and Website**

For the companies intending to put their business online, one of the biggest challenges they will face is to decide on who will launch and run the online store website. The companies can choose between two options, whether to hire a web developer to build and host their sites, or use an online hosting service that will build and maintain the online stores.

It will be expensive and difficult for e-commerce companies to operate and maintain its own websites. They need to invest in hardware, a dedicated Internet connection and software, along with a webmaster and programmers to maintain the site. This is a fairly important element since no customer will tolerate a buggy, unreliable online store. The companies can choose to pay a web hosting provider to build and maintain a deluxe, fully customized online store. Since the expense may be high, the e-commerce companies need to invest a huge amount of money in it. But they can enjoy professional web hosting services. The maintenance of the website will be left to the service providers too.

Website Features

E-commerce web pages may include the following contents.

Category Pages—These pages allow visitors to browse products organized by categories. The category pages will show small images of the products and prices that when clicked on will take the visitor to the product page. Visitors can also add products to their shopping basket directly from the category pages.

Product Pages—Each product in your e-commerce website will have its own

Remark

product page that contains a description of the produce, a larger image of the product and quantity box with an "add to basket" button.

Search Results Page—After a visitor completes a keyword search they will see this page that will allow the visitor to add any matching products to their basket or to view the matching products product pages.

Create/Edit Account—This feature allows visitors to create an account to save contact and shipping information. This provides a convenience so a returning customer will not have to re-enter their information when making a purchase. Existing customers can login to edit their account information. No credit card information is stored.

View Basket—This is the page that a customer sees after they have added a product to their basket. Here a visitor can change quantities and remove items as well as view their subtotal before taxes and shipping charges.

Checkout Pages—This is the checkout procedure. For example, it may have three steps. The first step is where the customer enters their contact and shipping information, the second is where a customer chooses their shipping and payment method and the third is where they enter their payment information. When the order is completed there is a confirmation page. An email is sent to both the merchant and the customer with every completed order.

Words and Expressions

register *v.*	注册
submit *v.*	提交
image *n.*	any picture 图像
consultant *n.*	顾问
credit card	信用卡
indicate *v.*	表明
manually *adv.*	手工的，人工的
bold *adj.*	黑体，粗体
insert *v.*	插入，填写
primer *n.*	入门书，初学者读物
icon *n.*	图标
italic *adj.*	斜体的
retrieve *v.*	取回，收回
clip art	剪贴画
Domain name	域名
Domain registrar	域名注册
FTP (file transfer protocol)	文件传输协议
GIF (graphics, interchange format)	图形交换格式

Remark

HTML (hypertext markup language)　　超文本链接语言
JPEG　　　　　　　　　　　　　图像的压缩编码格式

Notes

1. **TCP/IP** （transmission control protocol/Internet protocol）：It is the suite of protocols that defines the Internet. ICP/IP software is now included with every major kind of computer operating system. To be truly on the Internet，your computer must have TCP/IP software.

2. **IP Number** （Internet protocol number）：sometimes the IP number is called a dotted quad. A unique number consisting of 4 parts separated by dots，for example，165. 113. 245. 2. Every machine that is on the Internet has a unique IP number—if a machine does not have an IP number，it is not really on the internet. Many machines （especially servers） also have one or more Domain Names that are easier for people to remember.

3. **URL** （uniform resource locator）：It refers to the global address of documents and other resources on the World Wide Web. The first part of the address indicates what protocol to use，and the second part specifies the IP address or the domain name where the resource is located.

4. **Domain Name**：It is a name that identifies one or more IP addresses. For example，the domain name Microsoft. Com represents about a dozen IP addresses. Domain names are used in URLs to identify particular Web pages.

Exercises

Reading Comprehension

According to the text，answer the following questions.

1. According to the text，what do you need to make your web debut?

2. What is the relationship between the domain name and IP number?

3. Can you list more domain name suffixes?

4. Would you like to summarize the elements involved in making an effective online store website?

5. What does TCP/IP stand for?

Translation

A. Translate the following sentences into Chinese.

1. Of course，building an effective Web site requires a touch of artistic creativity and some energetic work to keep it fresh. Simple Web sites are straightforward to build and publish on a Web server.

2. Although it is possible to program Web pages manually using HTML tags, development software tools called Web editors can insert the tags for you, simplifying the task of coding home pages.

3. If you have the technical knowledge and some artistic talent, you can do it yourself.

4. When your browser requests a Web page stored at the server, the Web server sends the appropriate HTML and graphic files over the Internet to your machine for display on the screen.

5. For the companies intending to put their business online, one of the biggest challenges they will face is to decide on who will launch and run the online store website.

B. Translate the following sentences into English with the given words.

1. 航班晚点了几个小时，你托运的货物无法按时到达。(delay, as scheduled)

2. 我们很高兴就你的提案报价。(bid on)

3. 如果一个公司想要将产品加到目录里，只要改变数据就可以了。(add to)

4. 建立网站不仅需要计算机操作技术，而且需要一定的艺术创造力。(a touch of)

5. 你的图片资料占据了硬盘的大部分空间。(take up)

Supplementary Reading

Website

Building a website requires many basic stages. First, you must determine who is your audience? Is the site for children or adults? Does your audience access the Net from work, school or home? Do they want to be informed or entertained?

You site must be well organized, both for the benefit of your visitors and to make it easier to maintain.

Pay attention that a website is a perpetual work-progress. Most websites change fairly often because the technology makes electronic publishing rapid and relatively inexpensive. A well-planned site simplifies this process. New content and features can be easily added without having to redesign the site.

Second, the content of your site will be a combination of information that you currently have and that you will have to create. You may want to hire a creative writer, or for businesses, a Web-savvy public relations pro to help you put into writing some of the concepts inherent in your company and its products and services.

Third, no matter how well-organized and interesting your content is, graphics set the tone. You can create a good impression with some well designed graphics on the home page. Repeat a few design elements throughout the site to create a sense of continuity. A good designer can give you great help.

The most important thing to keep in mind in choosing graphic designers is to work with professionals who understand the unique requirements of the Web.

Once you have planned your site and created the content and graphics, you will need to convert your information into a Web-readable form. You can convert text documents to HTML and the graphics into GIF or JPEG format. If you have only a few pages to create, you can probably do it yourself. If you need help, you can hire an HTML coder.

When you begin working with forms, CGI scripts, image maps, or online transactions, you probably will need the services of a programmer. After all of your material is ready and you've got a programmer ready, you will need a place to host your site. Most individuals host their sites with their Internet service provider or with a web hosting company.

Fifth, promote your website is very import. Many web page developers seem to think that if you build a page, people will come. Unfortunately, with several billion pages on the Internet, the odds of someone bumping into yours is rather remote, unless it is well promoted. Web page promotion entails registering your URL with one or more search engines and portals.

A few very large search engines are used by most Internet users on a regular basis. You should certainly register your site with each of these.

Depending on your objectives, you may want to register with some of the international, regional or subject based search engines. You can add your URL to each major search engines by clicking below:

◆ Add URL to Yahoo!
◆ Add URL to Google

You can also use our free URL submission service to register your site with up to 18 search engines at once.

To statistically track visitors to your website is very important. Web tracking software provides a wealth of information about website visitors that can help you improve your web content, navigational structure and "stickiness". Good information will help you formulate great strategies that will ultimately lower your costs and increase your revenues.

It is important to use the information to refine your Meta tags and develop strategies that will improve your site's visibility in the major search engines.

Then, to maintain your website on a regular basis is essential. A fresh website encourages visitors to return again and again. A stale website will lead to a decrease in website traffic.

Last, you should manage your website feedback. Your website will generate emails, feedback response and sales leads. In order to ensure the information received can be acted upon in a timely manner, you should consider carefully who will

Remark

receive this information.

Notes

1. HTML 超文本标记语言
2. CGI 通用网关接口

Words and Expressions

perpetual *adj.*	永久性的
Web-savvy *adj.*	精通网络的
pro (professional) *n.*	专家，内行
inherent *adj.*	固有的
convert *v.*	转换
odds *n.*	几率
bump into	撞见
entail *v.*	包含
stale *adj*	陈旧的

A Guide to E-mail Writting

投诉 (complaints)

写作要点：首先指明出现的问题，并分析问题产生的原因以及严重的后果，然后提出解决问题的办法和建议。

Specimen Letter.

Dear Moyi,

Unfortunately our customer got angry and reject the furnace because it is used. . . .

The imprint of Heating Flame in the chamber is very clear.

In the beginning of this deal we are looking forward to a big co-operation with you. We even want to be your agent in Egypt，but now. . .

Dear Moyi，you know that I am a SALES DEP in the company，and the owner of my company order me to contact another person in your company to explain this problem. I will wait for your reply and explanation ASAP.

SALES DEP

AHMED ELMASRY

点评：这是一封来自埃及的投诉函，如果不能得到满意的答复似乎就要终止贸易关系，信的最后甚至没有用 Best regards 这样礼节性的词语结束。

- ASAP：是 as soon as possible 的缩写。

Unit 12 The Future of E-commerce

Warming-up Questions：

1. E-bay, a successful case in e-commerce, has attracted people all over the world. Would you like to give the reasons why e-Bay can become the crowd puller?

2. The advances in modern Internet technology greatly boost the development of e-commerce, which, in turn, brings dramatic changes to our life. What changes have you experienced in your life?

3. Can you predict the future trend of e-commerce?

Related links：

1. http：//www. computerworld. com/blogs/node/189
2. http：//pcquest. ciol. com/content/businesscomputing/102101102. asp

E-commerce—the Present

Since 1995, Internet users have witnessed the development of many innovative applications, ranging from online seals sales to e-learning experiences. Almost every medium—and large-sized organization in the world now has a Web site, and most MultiNational Corporation (MNC) have comprehensive portals through which employees, business partners, and the public can easily access corporate information in every corner of the globe. Many of these sites contain tens of thousands of pages and links, enabling the seamless flow of information to the audience.

E-commerce experienced a fast growing time in application. In 1999, the emphasis of EC shifted from B2C to B2B, and in 2001 from B2B to B2E, C-commerce, e-government, e-learning and m-commerce. Given the nature of technology and the Internet, EC will undoubtedly continue to shift and change. Today there is no place on the globe that EC has not reached , and we are seeing more and more EC successes around us.

During the last 10～15 years we have seen extremely successful virtual EC companies such as e-Bay, Amazon, and AOL. We also have seen major successes in click-and-mortar companies such as Cisco, GE, IBM, Intel and UPS. Yet, there are many success stories of start-up companies such as mtixtl. com, batteryspace. com, Drugstore. com, and campusfood. com.

Not every E-Commerll company has the luck to taste the happiness of success, starting in 1999 a large number of EC-dedicated companies, especially e-tailing ones, began to fail. The well-known B2C failures are eToys, Xpeditor, March-First, Webvan. com and Boo. com.

Does the large number of failures mean that EC's days are numbered? Absolutely not! First, the dot-com failure rate is declining sharply. Second , the EC field is basically experiencing consolidation, as companies test different business models and organizational structures. Third, most pure EC companies, including giants such as Amazon. com, are not yet making a profit or are making only small profits, but they are expanding operations and generating increasing sales. Some analysts predict that by 2004 many of the major pure EC companies will begin to generate profits.

E-commerce—the Future

In 1996 Forrester Research institute (forrester. com), a major EC-industry analyst, predicts that B2C would be a $6. 6 billion business in 2000, up from $518 million in 1996. In 2000, B2C sales in the United States actually were about $18 billion , or 1 percent of total retail sales. Today's predictions about future size of EC, provided by respected analysts such as AMR Research, Emarketer. com, and Forrester vary. For example, for 2004, total online shopping and B2B transaction in the United States are estimated to be in the range of $3 to $7 trillion. Experts predict that as many as 50 percent of all Internet users will shop online by that time. EC growth will come not only from B2C, but also from B2B and from newer applications such as e-government, e-learning, B2E, and c-commerce. Overall, the growth of the field will continue into the foreseeable future.

Words and Expressions

witness *v.*		见证
innovative *adj.*		革新的，创新的
comprehensive *adj.*		全面的，综合的
portal *n.*		壮观的大门
seamless *adj.*		无缝的
start-up companies		新成立的公司
consolidation *n.*		enhancing or making sth strong 巩固
virtual *adj.*		虚拟的
analyst *n.*		分析者
retail sales		零售

Remark

Notes

1. **click-and-mortar company**：鼠标加水泥，表示在网络上建立的虚拟店铺，即通过电子商务进行营销。

2. **brick-and-mortar**：砖头加水泥，表示在物理空间上建立实体性店铺，即我们通常所说的营销方式。

Exercises

Reading Comprehension

According to the text, answer the following questions.

1. E-commerce experienced a fast growing time in application. In 1999, the emphasis of EC shifted from B2C to B2B, and in 2001 from B2B to B2E, C-commerce, e-government, e-learning and m-commerce. Would you like to give the reasons why E-commerce is experiencing the shift?

2. What drives the author to the assumption that in the future E-commerce will continue to shift and change?

3. In the article, some successful stories about e-commerce are put forth. Can you name more cases like this?

4. What does "click-and-mortar companies" mean? Try to explain the term in your own words.

5. Experts predict that as many as 50 percent of all Internet users will shop online by that time. Do you agree with the statement? Use statistics to support your viewpoint.

Case Study

The Success Story of *Campusfood*. *com*

Campusfood's recipe for success was a simple one: providing interactive menus to college students, using the power of the internet to replace and /or facilitate the traditional telephone ordering of meals. Launched at the University of Pennsylvania (Penn), the company is taking thousands of orders each month for local restaurants, bringing pizzas, hoagies, and wings to Penn community and to dozens of other universities.

Founder Michael Saunders began developing the site (campusfood. com) in 1997 while he was a junior at Penn. With the help of some classmates, Saunders launched the site in 1998. After graduation, he began building the company's customer base. This involved expanding to other universities, attracting students, and generating a list of restaurants from which students could order food for delivery.

Currently, some of these activities are outsourced to a marketing firm, enabling the addition of dozens of schools nationwide.

Financed through private investors, friends, and family members, the site was built on an investment of less than $1 million. (For comparison, another company with services also reaching the college student market invested $100 million.) Campusfood. com's revenue is generated through transaction fees—the site takes a 5 percent commission on each order from the sellers (the restaurants).

Questions for discussion:

1. Classify this application by the use of E-commerce transaction type.

2. Explain the benefits of Campuusfood. com for its student customers and for the restaurants it represents.

3. Trace the flow of digitized information in this venture.

4. How does the outsourcing of the marketing activities contribute to the business?

Translation

A. Translate the following sentences into Chinese.

1. Since 1995, Internet users have witnessed the development of many innovative applications, ranging from online seals sales to e-learning experiences.

2. Many of these sites contain tens of thousands of pages and links, enabling the seamless flow of information to the audience.

3. Given the nature of technology and the Internet, EC will undoubtedly continue to shift and change.

4. Today's predictions about future size of EC, provided by respected analysts such as AMR Research, Emarketer. com, and Forrester vary.

5. Does the large number of failures mean that EC's days are numbered?

B. Translate the following sentences into English with the given words.

1. 近几年人们见证了网络的迅猛发展。(witness)

2. 研究者们正在摸索创新性的传送信息的方法。(innovative)

3. 考虑到环境的情况，你的公司已经做得很好了。(given)

4. 这家房地产公司在这笔交易中赚取了高额利润。(make a profit)

Supplementary Reading

The Prospect of E-commerce

Today improvements in web site design and functionality combined with high speed broadband Internet connections greatly improve the online shopping experience, while improvements in Internet security and increasing public awareness has helped to boost consumer confidence. And a better understanding of Internet mar-

Remark

keting and SEO allows small business owners to successfully market their e-commerce business within the rapidly growing e-commerce industry.

The Internet is now a functional medium for consumers, information seekers, business owners and entrepreneurs. According to recent surveys during upcoming 5 years, e-commerce will develop very fast and retail sales in US are expected to take off: it will grow annually on about $20 billion to $30 billion and by 2012 will reach, at least, $215 billion. The highest level is $335 billion. In view of 2007 indexes demonstrated 21% increase over 2006 these predictions don't seem so fantastic.

Forrester Research Inc in its report "U. S. E-Commerce Forecast: 2008 to 2012" cites the following figures: online retail sales will reach $204 billion in 2008, $235.4 billion in 2009, $267.8 billion in 2010, $301 billion in 2011, and $334.7 billion in 2012. Jupiter Research LLC in its "U. S. Online Retail Forecast, 2007-2012" has presented decent numbers: in 2008 non-travel-related e-commerce will reach $148 billion, $166 billion in 2009, $182 billion in 2010, $199 billion in 2011, and $215 billion in 2012.

What drove and will drive this increase? With rapid improvements in Internet technologies and increased public awareness, more shoppers are realizing the benefits of shopping online.

The main reasons more shoppers went to the Internet for their shopping are convenience avoiding crowds, more variety , and better bargains.

In spite of the amazing numbers and the benefits drawn from online shopping, the statistics shows that customers prefer real stores leaving virtual shopping as seasonably. So, retails are faced with the problem how to improve their activity and to increase the traffic and online sales. Now they need to take some steps to ensure their Web sites are more conducive to browsing. Also retailers should widely use up-to-date technologies and provide with more information on their goods. Flexibility in payment and returns are also a good tool to attract online customers.

Besides all these, user reviews and peer comments are more likely to generate online shopping revenue than traditional advertising. According to eMarketer, social shopping on sites that offers a forum for users to conduct web chat about products, services and providers plays an increasingly prominent role in e-commerce.

Where's it Going?

Increasing availability of broadband Internet services combined with new applications and marketing research will allow e-commerce sales to rise for years to come. Currently 50% of the households in the United States have broadband access, and as this percentage increases this rapid e-commerce growth will continue. The Internet is now delivering what we expected from it several years ago. Getting into e-commerce today is still considered

Remark

the ground floor. Maybe it's time for your idea.

Notes

SEO (search engine optimization) 意思是搜索引擎优化

Words and Expressions

boost	v.	推进
entrepreneur	n.	企业家
take off		复制
bargain	n.	讨价还价
prominent	adj.	突出的
availability	n.	可利用性、可得到性

A guide to E-mail Writting

发票（invoice）

HEFEI KEJING MATERIALS TECHNOLOGY CO.，LTD.

Tel：86-551-5591559　　　　Fax：86-551-5592689

Email：kmt@aiofm.ac.cn　　　　Web site：www.kmtcrystal.com

INVOICE

To：Division of Physics & Applied Physics

School of Physical & Mathemaical Science.　QUOTATION NO.：20070917

Nanyang Technological University　　　　DATE：17-Sept-2007

ADDRESS：60 Nanyang Drive，SBS B3N-04，Singapore 637551

　　　　　　　　　　　　　　　　　　PAGE：1 of 1

ATTN：Asst. Prof. Wang Lan/Dr. Huang Shengli

TEL：+65-6316 2964　　　FAX：+65-6794 1325

Item	Description	Quantity	Unit Price (CIF Sigapore) (US $/pc)	Amount (US $)
1	$LaAlO_3$,<100>,10x3x0.4~0.5mm,1sp	10	4.30	43
2	$LaSrAlO_4$,<100>,10x3x0.4~0.5mm,1sp	10	10.80	108
3	$LaSrAlO_4$,<001>,10x3x0.4~0.5mm,1sp	10	8.80	88
4	MgO,<100>,10x3x0.4~0.5mm,1sp	10	4.80	48
5	$SrTiO_3$,<100>,10x3x0.4~0.5mm,1sp	10	8.30	83
6	YSZ,<111>,5x5x0.5mm,1sp	20	3.00	60
7	YSZ,<100>,5x5x0.5mm,1sp	20	3.00	60
	Freight	1	50.00	50
	TOTAL			USD540

NOTE：

Beneficial bank information：

HEFEI HIGH&NEW TECHNOLOGY INDUSTRIAL DEVELOPMENT ZONE

BRANCH，BANK OF CHINA

Beneficiary：HEFEI DEJING MATERIALS TECHNOLOGY CO.，LTD

Bank address：Changjiang west road No. 669，Hefei City，Anhui Province，P. R. China

Post code：230088

Account No：01329908093014

Swift No.：BKCHCNBJA780

PAYMENT：_____Advanced payment by T/T_____

SHIPPING DATE：_____1 week after PO confirmed_____

DESTINATION：_____Singapore_____

PACKAGE：_____Box_____

VALIDITY：_____60 days_____

_____
Signature & Stamp

点评：通常在发货 3～5 天后可以向收货单位寄发 INVOICE，切记不要发得太早，那样很不礼貌。INCOICE 就相当我们常用的发票。收货方将根据 invoice 提供的信息付款。Advance payment by T/T（telegraphic transfer）提前电付。LaAlO$_3$：铝酸镧，SrTiO$_3$ 钛酸锶，MgO 氧化镁，单晶，是目前超导学科研究领域使用最普遍的材料。

Reference

[1] Efraim Turban，David King. Electronic Commerce—A. Manageral perspective. 北京：高等教育出版社，2006.

[2] Dr. Bruce J. Mclaren，Dr. Constance H. Mclaren. E-commerce Basics. Thomson，2003.

Remark